A Framework to Evaluate Proposals for Scientific Activities in Wilderness

United States Department of Agriculture

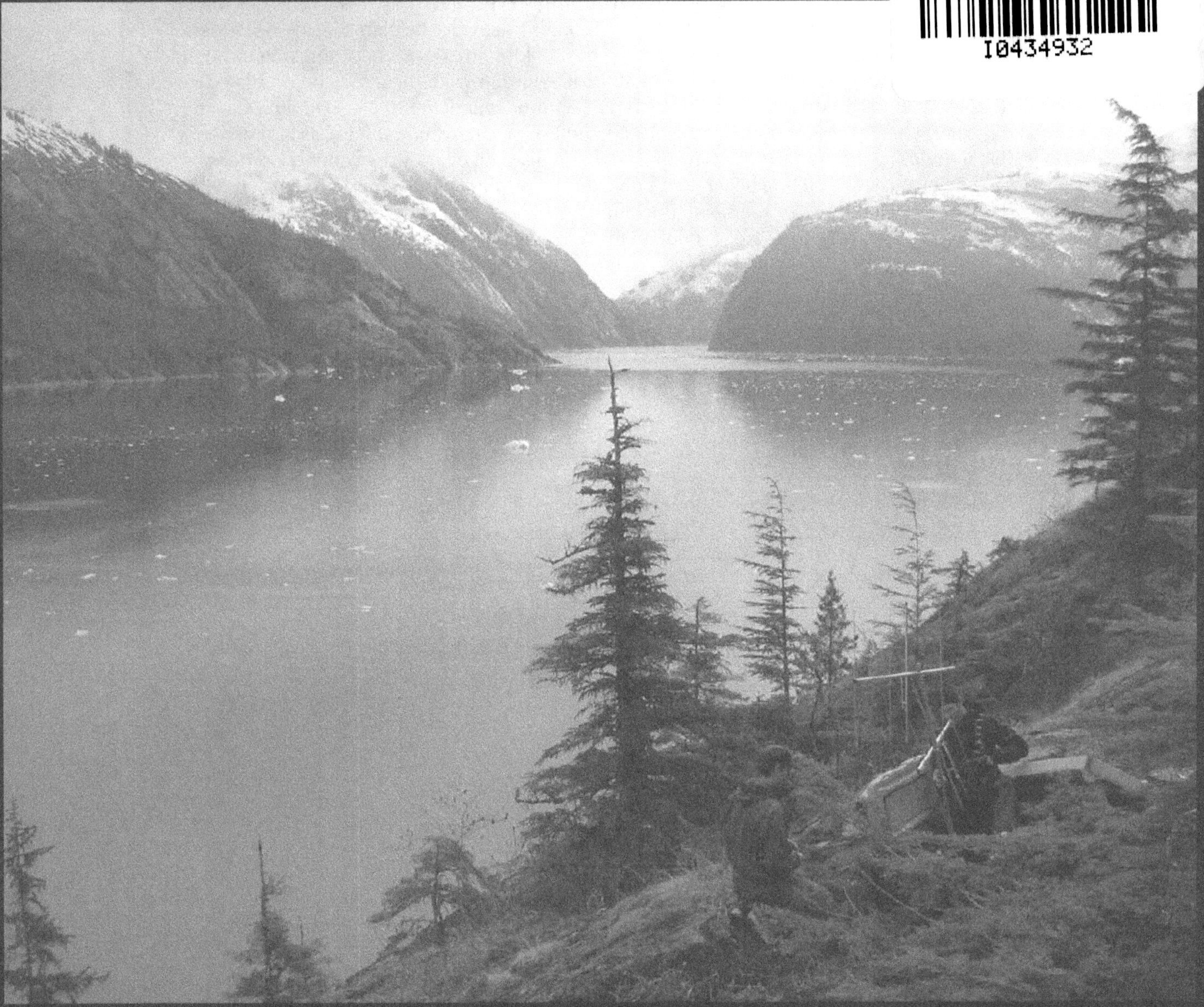

Forest Service

Rocky Mountain Research Station

General Technical Report RMRS-GTR-234WWW

January 2010

Abstract

Every year, the four Federal wilderness management agencies—U.S. DOI Bureau of Land Management, Fish and Wildlife Service, National Park Service, and the USDA Forest Service—receive hundreds of proposals to conduct scientific studies within wilderness. There is no consistent and comprehensive framework for evaluating such proposals that accounts for the unique legal requirements of conducting such work inside wilderness, specifically the primary mandate of the 1964 Wilderness Act to "preserve wilderness character." This mandate demands that the standard for approving scientific activities be higher inside wilderness than in other areas. This evaluation framework provides an approach for thinking through and documenting how proposals for scientific activities in wilderness may be evaluated in these wilderness management agencies based on four sequential filters: (1) Initial Review Filter, (2) Quality of Proposal Filter, (3) Legal and Policy Filter, and (4) Impacts and Benefits Filter. By using this framework, managers and scientists alike know up-front how proposals will be evaluated, fostering better communication. This framework aims to reduce conflict, help make defensible decisions, and document how those decisions are made. Our goals in developing this framework are to increase the relevance of science to improving wilderness stewardship and to bring the benefits of wilderness to society while preserving wilderness character.

Keywords: wilderness, scientific activities, scientific evaluation, wilderness permitting

Authors

Peter Landres is an Ecologist at the Aldo Leopold Wilderness Research Institute, Rocky Mountain Research Station, USDA Forest Service, Missoula, MT.

Mark Fincher is the Wilderness Specialist at Yosemite National Park, National Park Service, El Portal, CA.

Lewis Sharman is an Ecologist at Glacier Bay National Park and Preserve, National Park Service, Gustavus, AK.

Judy Alderson is the Regional Wilderness Program Manager, Alaska Regional Office, National Park Service, Anchorage, AK.

Chris Barns is the Bureau of Land Management representative at the Arthur Carhart National Wilderness Training Center, Missoula, MT.

Tom Carlson is the USDA Forest Service representative at the Arthur Carhart National Wilderness Training Center, Missoula, MT.

Richard L. Anderson is the Compliance Coordinator at the Alaska Regional Office, National Park Service, Anchorage, AK.

Susan Boudreau is the Superintendent at Klondike Gold Rush National Historic Park, National Park Service, Skagway, AK.

David J. Parsons is the Director of the Aldo Leopold Wilderness Research Institute, Rocky Mountain Research Station, USDA Forest Service, Missoula, MT.

Laurel Boyers (retired) was formerly the Wilderness Manager at Yosemite National Park, National Park Service, El Portal, CA.

Kevin Hood is the Coordinator for Special Uses/Wilderness/Outdoor Ethics (LNT) at Admiralty Island National Monument and the Juneau Ranger District of the Tongass National Forest, Juneau, AK.

Author's Note: This publication was developed by a technical working group and solely represents the views of its authors. It does not represent and should not be construed to represent any agency determination or policy.

Acknowledgments

This framework was initially developed through a 2001 interagency workshop. We are indebted to the participants: Robin West and Danny Gomez (U.S. Fish and Wildlife Service); Bruce Van Haveren (Bureau of Land Management); Steve Bair, John Dennis, and David Graber (National Park Service); Dan Fagre (U.S. Geological Survey); and Kendall Clark and John Romanowski (USDA Forest Service).

We thank the participants, especially Allison Banks and Greg Streveler, in a workshop held at Glacier Bay National Park and Preserve to develop an initial working model of this framework. We thank Tomie Lee, former Park superintendent, for her support and encouragement.

Joe Van Horn, Wilderness Program Coordinator for Denali National Park and Preserve, was instrumental in keeping our feet to the wilderness fire. Rob Mason, a former wilderness manager for the Forest Service, offered thoughtful advice on ways to make this evaluation framework more practical and useful to wilderness managers. Many other people offered cogent comments and suggestions, including Paul Gleeson, Gordon Olson, and the many workshop and discussion participants at several biennial George Wright Society meetings where previous drafts of this framework were presented.

We thank Rick Potts, former Chief of Wilderness Stewardship and Recreation Management in the National Park Service, for his unflagging support and encouragement. And we sincerely appreciate all the members of the National Park Service's National Wilderness Steering Committee (now Wilderness Leadership Council) for their sustained interest and assistance in reviewing and revising this framework. We are especially grateful to Bob Winfree, National Park Service Alaska Regional Science Advisor, for sharing his depth of experience and for his help, support, and feedback throughout the many stages of developing this evaluation framework. David Graber, Chief Scientist for the Pacific West Region of the National Park Service, and Steve Ulvi (now retired from the National Park Service) were constant sources of wisdom, support, and humor to help us think through many difficult issues and decisions and to keep us focused on how to simultaneously support science and preserve wilderness character.

Table of Contents

Executive Summary

This evaluation framework provides a consistent and comprehensive approach for thinking through and documenting how the four Federal wilderness managing agencies may evaluate proposals for scientific activities in wilderness. This approach is based on the premises that both impacts and benefits need to be assessed and that the decision to approve or deny a proposed activity ultimately depends on whether the benefits justify the impacts. Such an approach provides a solid basis to improve communication between managers and scientists, thereby reducing conflict and impacts to wilderness character, increasing the relevance of science to improving wilderness stewardship, and bringing the benefits of wilderness science to society.

Why is this evaluation framework needed?

The standard for approving scientific activities is, and should be, set higher inside wilderness than in other areas because of the legislative requirement from the 1964 Wilderness Act to "preserve wilderness character." However, there is no consistent and comprehensive framework for evaluating proposals for scientific activities in wilderness. Different agencies, and offices within an agency, may evaluate proposals differently and interpret the requirements of wilderness legislation as well as agency policy in very different ways. Typically, some impacts but not others are evaluated, while the benefits of the proposed work may or may not be taken into account. Last, the trigger for more detailed evaluation often is a proposed action that is prohibited by Section 4(c) of the Wilderness Act, and, while many scientific activities may not reach that level of impact, they may still have a significant impact on wilderness character. All of these habits lead to a lack of defensibility when approving or denying proposals, as well as frustration and acrimony between managers and scientists. These problems will likely become more frequent and intense with increasing demands for research and monitoring in wilderness to understand the effects of global climate change and other pervasive, regional, and national-scale threats to wilderness.

How does this evaluation framework work?

This framework consists of a series of steps or filters that would typically be used in the following sequence to reach a recommendation about the proposal:

- *Initial Review Filter:* identify any potential "red flags" or obvious problems
- *Quality of Proposal Filter:* ensure the activities will achieve their intended outcome
- *Legal and Policy Filter:* evaluate conformance with existing legislation and applicable agency policies
- *Impacts and Benefits Filter:* evaluate both impacts and benefits

One of the purposes of this framework is to quickly identify proposals that may be readily approved, those that are clearly not appropriate and will be returned with an explanation, and those that will require substantial effort to render a fair and transparent decision. While the framework may at first seem complex, extensive pilot testing showed that, using this framework, most proposals, after they have been carefully read, require about 15 minutes to evaluate.

This framework applies to proposals from inside the wilderness management agency and to proposals from other agencies, organizations, and individuals. This framework is not intended for off-the-shelf use. Local staffs are required to make several judgments within the filters described above, and these judgments strongly influence the outcome of this evaluation. This framework is not intended to be prescriptive; rather, to balance the goals of consistency and local relevance, it provides a logical structure within which staffs apply specific modifications to fit local circumstances.

This framework will assist in the preparation of a National Environmental Policy Act analysis, as well as a Minimum Requirements Analysis, if needed, but it is not a substitute for either. Each agency and managing unit uses different procedures for triggering and fulfilling compliance requirements, so each will need to develop its own methods for incorporating this framework into compliance procedures.

A Framework to Evaluate Proposals for Scientific Activities in Wilderness

Peter Landres, Mark Fincher, Lewis Sharman, Judy Alderson,
Chris Barns, Tom Carlson, Richard L. Anderson, Susan Boudreau,
David J. Parsons, Laurel Boyers, and Kevin Hood

Introduction

Every year, the four Federal wilderness management agencies (U.S. DOI Bureau of Land Management, Fish and Wildlife Service, National Park Service, and the USDA Forest Service) receive hundreds of proposals to conduct scientific studies within wilderness. These proposals range from simple and small to extraordinarily complex and large projects. Wilderness offers unique opportunities for biophysical and social science in areas that are relatively unmodified by modern people, and these studies may improve wilderness stewardship and benefit both science and society (Albright 1933; Bratton 1988; Graber 1988, 2002; Peterson 1996; Sharman and others 2007; Suarez 2009). The legislative requirement of the 1964 Wilderness Act to "preserve wilderness character" demands that the standard for approving scientific activities is, and should be, set higher inside wilderness than in other areas (Landres and others 2003; Six and others 2000).

Some scientific activities in wilderness are illegal because wilderness legislation prohibits motorized equipment, mechanical transport, and installations. These prohibitions prevent the use of certain scientific tools, data collection installations, and other scientific procedures unless these are explicitly deemed "necessary to meet minimum requirements for the administration of the area for the purpose of this Act" (Section 4(c) Wilderness Act, Public Law 88-577). Other activities may be legal but, nonetheless, diminish one or more of the four qualities of wilderness character (see Landres and others 2008 for detailed discussion about wilderness character). For example, the presence of research staff compromises opportunities for solitude, monumentation of research sites with permanent marking diminishes the undeveloped quality, and tagging animals compromises the untrammeled quality of wilderness character (for additional examples, see Oelfke and others 2000; Parsons 2000; Parsons and Graber 1991).

Different agencies, and even different offices within an agency, may interpret wilderness legislation and the agency's policies in different ways, leading to inconsistency in evaluating proposals for scientific activities (Butler and Roberts 1986). This inconsistency, combined with a lack of communication between managers and scientists, has led to increasing frustration and

USDA Forest Service Gen. Tech. Rep. RMRS-GTR-234WWW. 2010

1

acrimony over scientific activities in wilderness (Barns 2000; Bayless 1999; Eichelberger and Sattler 1994; Stokstad 2001). For example, Franklin (1987) describes how scientists "are often uninformed about regulations and unwilling to make necessary compromises to conform with wilderness values. Scientists can be arrogant and cryptic in their relations with managers...some may feel that research gives them a license to do whatever they please." Franklin (1987) also describes how managers' "attitudes toward research in wilderness are also problems...which may include hostility and disinterest, [and] apparently reflect a lack of appreciation of the potential value of scientific study." These problems will likely become more frequent and intense with increasing demands for research and monitoring in wilderness to understand the effects of global climate change and other pervasive, regional, and national-scale threats to wilderness. Appendix A offers an example of how this evaluation framework relates specifically to climate change research and Appendix B offers guidelines for scientists developing proposals to conduct research in wilderness.

To help overcome these problems, this framework was developed to provide a consistent approach across the four wilderness management agencies for thinking through and documenting how proposals for scientific activities in wilderness may be evaluated. Our premises include: (1) there is nothing inherently incompatible between science and wilderness; (2) science can substantively contribute to improved wilderness stewardship and societal understanding about the value of wilderness; and (3) both impacts and benefits of proposed scientific activities must be fairly evaluated to decide whether to approve or deny these activities. This framework should both set the stage for discussion between managers and scientists early in the proposal development process and be equally informative and useful to both groups. By improving communication between managers and scientists, this framework aims to reduce conflict, increase the relevance of science to improving wilderness stewardship, and help bring the benefits of wilderness science to society, while preserving wilderness character.

This framework was initially developed at a workshop held in 2001 with the four wilderness management agencies and the U.S. Geological Survey. This initial framework was presented at several conference discussions and workshops, and an intensive workshop was held at Glacier Bay National Park and Preserve in 2005. The framework was then substantially revised by the present authors, again presented at a conference workshop, and subsequently revised and pilot tested.

Evaluation Framework Goals

The general goals for this framework are to:

- *Improve communication*—There is a fundamental need to have early and clear communication between scientists and management staff about how proposals for scientific activities in wilderness will be evaluated.

- *Improve awareness*—There is an important need to improve awareness and understanding among both scientists and management staff about (1) the importance of preserving wilderness character, protecting the wilderness resource, and the high standard that is required for conducting scientific studies in wilderness; and (2) the direct and indirect benefits of science to wilderness and its stewardship and to society.

- *Improve defensibility*—There is an urgent need to improve the defensibility of staff evaluations by using a framework that is (1) transparent and explicit in the decision criteria, including the subjective judgments made by agency staff; (2) based on the statutory language of the 1964 Wilderness Act; and (3) consistent in its evaluation criteria across different proposals and over time. Such an evaluation framework would become part of the administrative record demonstrating how a decision was made.

To accomplish these goals, this framework is designed to be:

- *Comprehensive and systematic*—The framework provides a structured basis for comprehensively evaluating the benefits and impacts of a proposed scientific activity, including the cumulative benefits and impacts of this activity.

- *Broadly applicable*—The framework applies to every geographic area and agency because it is based on the statutory language of the 1964 Wilderness Act.

- *Flexible*—The framework has been designed to allow local modification. In fact, local modification is required in several places to ensure that decisions reflect local thinking and attitudes about wilderness and science.

Limitations and Cautions

There are several limitations and cautions about the use of this framework. First, it was developed to evaluate proposals for scientific activities, not other types of activities such as outfitter and guide permits. Scientific activities are defined as all activities related to the collection of natural resource and social science data, including research, inventory, and monitoring, generally conducted by universities, Federal or State agencies, or private organizations. Second, significant portions of this framework are based on the statutory language of the 1964 Wilderness Act, and, therefore, it applies just to wilderness and not other agency lands. Third, this framework is intended to apply equally to proposals that come from outside or inside the Federal agency managing the wilderness. Fourth, the framework does not specifically evaluate impacts to the intangible aspects of wilderness character, such as impacts to humility, restraint, and the value of having areas that remain a mystery and unknown (Landres 2005), in other words, the virtue of having what Leopold (1949) described as "a blank spot on the map." These intangible values may be considered important by management staff in this evaluation process.

While this framework is intended to be widely applicable and useful, it is not prescriptive and local staffs must adapt and modify it to fit their needs. As with all management tools, the use of this framework needs to be tested within the legal and policy context of the specific wilderness and the circumstances being evaluated. In particular, this framework must be used with a clear understanding of wilderness values and the ability to translate this understanding to a variety of complex proposals and situations. This framework is intended to build upon and complement the knowledge and experience of local management staffs, not to serve as a substitute for this knowledge. Despite the benefits of a standardized evaluation process, no single evaluation process will work in every situation, especially in cases that have become contentious and politicized. Last, this framework is not a policy or decision document, and, while it may complement a minimum tool analysis and NEPA scoping and analysis documents, it does not replace either of those if needed.

To fully implement this framework, each agency will need to develop agency-specific approaches not provided here to:

- Identify appropriate staff roles and responsibilities;
- Integrate this framework within existing agency policies and permitting or approval programs, and make it part of the administrative record;
- Determine the appropriate balance between flexibility and consistency among different offices within an agency;
- Develop communication tools such as a Web-based application to provide a user's guide to this framework; and
- Develop supporting documentation to improve communication between management staff and scientists that would (1) explain why wilderness character is important and the Federal responsibility to preserve it, (2) provide examples of activities that are allowed and those that are prohibited, and (3) offer recommendations for sampling, monumentation, and other activities that are likely to cause concern.

Over 30 different proposals for scientific studies have been pilot-tested using an earlier draft of this framework. This version reflects what has been learned from that testing. Not surprisingly, pilot testing showed that familiarity with the framework is critical for efficient evaluation of a proposal. In particular, familiarity is needed with the numerical scoring system used to assess impacts. Understanding the details of a proposal also may require considerable time and effort, especially for complex proposals. However, once the evaluator understands the material, on average, proposals are evaluated in about 15 minutes.

Compliance Requirements

All Federal actions that might have an environmental effect are subject to the National Environmental Policy Act of 1970 (NEPA). Effects on wilderness character from scientific activities are subject to NEPA, and the conduct of these activities is under the control of the managing Federal agency and is therefore considered a Federal action. This is true whether the Federal wilderness management agency, another Federal agency, a State agency, a State or private university or museum, or an individual conducts the activities. This is also true regardless of whether a research permit is required. If no research permit is required, the agency still has the responsibility for wilderness management and for NEPA analysis of the scientific activities and impacts.

This evaluation framework, like any Minimum Requirements Analysis (MRA), may help prepare a NEPA analysis but is not a substitute. Portions of the evaluation framework, like the MRA, may be transferable to a subsequent or concurrent NEPA analysis. Because agencies and managing units use different procedures for triggering and fulfilling compliance requirements, no standard method is offered for how this framework should be incorporated into these compliance procedures.

To summarize the differences between this evaluation framework, the MRA, and NEPA:

- *Evaluation framework*—used to evaluate all scientific activities regardless of whether they are prohibited under the Wilderness Act Section 4(c) or not; evaluates both impacts and benefits of a proposed activity and weighs these against one another in the context of cumulative effects from other activities.
- *MRA*—used to evaluate the necessity of a proposed activity and how to minimize impacts from it, especially an activity that violates the Wilderness Act Section 4(c) prohibitions.
- *NEPA*—compares and discloses the environmental effects of all the alternatives, including the proposal and the no-action alternative.

Evaluation Framework Overview

The framework is composed of four filters or steps (fig. 1), followed by a recommendation about the proposed activity. The purpose of each step is briefly explained below and explained in detail in its own section.

- *Initial Review Filter*—identify any potential "red flags" and obvious problems with the proposal
- *Quality of Proposal Filter*—ensure the proposed activities will achieve their intended outcome
- *Legal and Policy Filter*—evaluate conformance of the proposal with existing legislation and applicable agency policies
- *Impacts and Benefits Filter*—assess the impacts and benefits of the proposal, including cumulative impacts
- *Recommendation*—the final recommendation that is rendered from the evaluation process

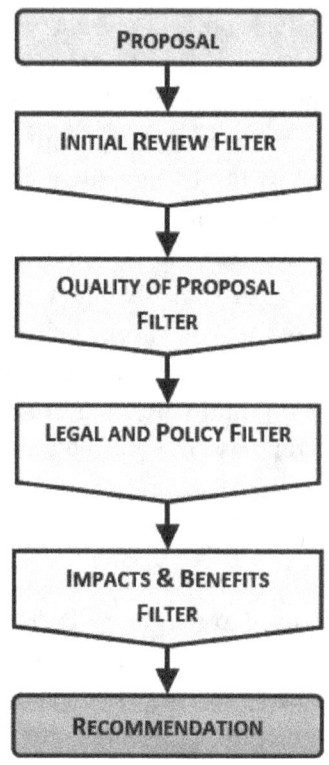

Figure 1—Overall evaluation process.

Throughout this evaluation framework we use the term "proposal" to refer to the entire document that is submitted to the agency for permitting and "proposed activity" for specific components of the proposal. In reality, it will most likely be one or more components of a proposal that end up being the primary focus of scrutiny and debate. For example, a proposal for climate change research may include the installation of a meteorological tower as one of its proposed activities, and this tower would likely become the focus of the Legal and Policy Filter. This framework is designed to be conservative by allowing a proposal to be provisionally denied at each of the different steps. In most cases, denial is provisional because agency staff would first document the reason for denial and may then negotiate with the scientist to reduce the impacts and/or increase the benefits of the proposal.

Any evaluation process, including this one, strives to put complex and nuanced issues into relatively simple categories or into black and white terms. For example, in this framework a proposal would be readily approved if it is of sufficient quality to achieve its intended purpose, does not violate law or policy, and does not degrade wilderness character. In contrast, a proposal would be readily denied if it is of poor quality, violated law or policy, or degraded wilderness character without providing any significant benefits. These are both simple situations and many proposals would fall into one or the other category. Much more complex and harder to evaluate, however, is a proposal that is of

USDA Forest Service Gen. Tech. Rep. RMRS-GTR-234WWW. 2010

6

good quality, would provide important benefits, but requires the use of Section 4(c) prohibited activities, and, therefore, degrades wilderness character to achieve those benefits. Should such a proposal be denied or approved after appropriate negotiation? This framework is intended to help managers evaluate these "gray" situations in a consistent and comprehensive manner, leading to fair and defensible decisions.

Initial Review Filter

The first step in this evaluation framework is to identify any potential "red flags" or other obvious problems with the proposal. For every wilderness and issue there will likely be a different set of "hot-button" issues that need to be identified as early and as quickly as possible. The purpose of this filter is not to deny a proposal but to set up appropriate management review if needed, or return it for modification to correct obvious problems before further evaluation. The mere presence of this filter should provide a strong incentive for scientists to talk with the wilderness manager *while* they are developing their proposal and certainly *before* the proposal is formally submitted. Such upfront communication may forestall any problems or antagonism that might prevent the proposal from being approved and, thereby, increase the speed of the evaluation process.

This filter is simply a list of questions management staff should ask about each proposal. The questions offered below illustrate the kinds of questions that would trigger a red flag, but this list may not cover the full range of issues or concerns that are relevant to a specific area or proposal. Similarly, this list may include questions that are not relevant to an area. These questions include:

- Does the proposal include any activities requiring a use that is legally prohibited by Section 4(c) of the Wilderness Act?
- Would the proposed activity degrade wilderness character even if it is legally permitted?
- Would the proposed activity likely be controversial with any publics?
- Would the proposed activity pose other legal or policy problems?
- Would the proposed activity interfere with management operations?
- Would the proposed activity pose consultation issues over listed species or cultural and heritage resources?
- Would the proposed activity require collecting plants or other natural resources, handling or removing animals, or introducing plants or animals into the wilderness?
- Would the proposed activity pose timing or location problems, such as occurring in a sensitive area or time for particular species?
- Would the proposed activity pose additional impact in an area that already has an unacceptable level of cumulative impacts or is close to an unacceptable level of cumulative impacts?

USDA Forest Service Gen. Tech. Rep. RMRS-GTR-234WWW. 2010

7

- If the submitter has conducted work in the area before, were there any problems with completing administrative requirements (such as submitting reports, removing installations and other debris from the activity, or completing curatorial and specimen documentation requirements) in a timely and professional manner?

The intent in managers asking these questions at the outset of the evaluation process is not to go into a thorough and deep analysis of potential problems. Rather, asking these questions is important to identify whether the proposal may trigger certain problems that could substantially influence how the proposal will be evaluated. For example, if the proposal affects threatened and endangered species, consultation with the U.S. Fish and Wildlife Service is required, which may lead to a longer evaluation. Likewise, if the proposal requires use of motorized equipment or mechanical transport or degrades wilderness character in some other way, the evaluation process may take longer and there is a greater chance it will be denied.

If the answer to any of these questions is "yes," then additional effort is needed by the manager to more clearly define what the potential problem is. At this point communication with the persons who offered the proposal is vital to inform them of the potential problem(s) and likely implications for how long it may take to evaluate their proposal. If this Initial Review Filter turns up problems that may significantly delay the evaluation or make it more likely for the proposal to be denied, management staff may allow the proposal to be withdrawn or revised. If the answer is "no" to all of the questions, then the proposal would advance to the next step in this framework.

Quality of Proposal Filter

This filter asks two questions:

- Is the proposed scientific activity sufficiently well designed to accomplish its stated purpose, thereby providing the intended benefits to management or science?
- Does the proposal adequately describe and discuss the potential benefits and impacts of the proposed activity to wilderness, as well as its plan for communicating with local management staff?

It is neither the wilderness manager's responsibility to understand research design, sampling methods, or statistical analysis, nor the scientist's responsibility to understand the intricacies and nuances of wilderness law and policy. With this filter and the two questions above, we are trying to forge common ground that both groups need to move toward. For example, wilderness managers need an informed opinion about whether the proposed activity will fulfill its intended objectives. For proposals that have little or no impact, this is not a crucial analysis. But for proposals that degrade wilderness character or require activities prohibited by Section 4(c) of the Wilderness Act, this evaluation is

USDA Forest Service Gen. Tech. Rep. RMRS-GTR-234WWW. 2010

8

imperative to accurately assess whether the purported benefits would be sufficient to justify accepting the impacts.

Managers typically have four options for evaluating scientific rigor: (1) review the proposal themselves if they are capable; (2) ask agency resource or science staff to review the proposal; (3) ask scientists outside the agency for review; or (4) assume that the proposal is sufficiently well-designed that no review is needed. The drawbacks to the first three options are the staff time and funding needed to review proposals. While the fourth option may appear specious, some national-level agency activities such as the Forest Service's Forest Inventory and Analysis program are developed with rigorous standards, and, in these cases, may not need to be reviewed for scientific quality. In some cases, the reputation of the person submitting the proposal or the manager's direct experience with this person may lead to accepting the scientific rigor of the proposal with minimal additional review.

In some cases, a proposal may be funded before it is submitted to the agency for approval to conduct the study on public land. For example, scientists may submit proposals to be funded by the National Science Foundation or special congressionally funded initiatives that have well-established independent review processes. In these cases, if the proposal has passed the rigorous screening of such programs, the scientific quality of the proposal may not need to be questioned. Having already received funding, however, neither assures that a proposal will be permitted nor exempts it from being assessed in the Legal and Policy Filter and the Impacts and Benefits Filter.

If the proposal is deemed inadequate to fulfill its intended scientific purpose, it may be returned with a request to demonstrate, by independent reviews, the scientific quality of the proposal.

The second question in this Filter evaluates whether the proposal adequately describes its potential benefits and impacts to wilderness, as well as its plan for communicating with local management staff. Specifically, reviewers should ask:

- Does the proposal describe the potential benefits as described in the Impacts and Benefits Filter?
- Does the proposal describe the potential impacts as described in the Impacts and Benefits Filter and show how these will be minimized or mitigated?
- Does the proposal describe how the results and any reports will be communicated to local management staff?

By describing the potential benefits of the activity, the proposal helps managers understand the broader context of the proposed activities. By describing potential impacts, the proposal demonstrates that the persons suggesting the activities are aware of the range of wilderness values that might be affected by their proposal. If the proposal does not address these issues, or addresses them inadequately, the proposal may be returned for revision. In this case, it is clearly in the scientist's interest to revise the proposal to increase the likelihood of it being permitted.

In some cases, managers may feel that the impacts are unacceptable and suggest ways the scientist could reduce them. For example, if a researcher proposes using a chainsaw to take sections from trees to develop an historical record of fire in the wilderness, the manager may support the idea for such a study and suggest that a crosscut saw be used instead. The scientist may counter that a chainsaw is necessary to provide the quality and quantity of data needed to derive an historical fire record, and the chainsaw allows plunge cutting that minimizes tree damage. The manager may then respond that a chainsaw can be used but only in certain times and locations to minimize impacts to visitors. In addition, the manager may seek the opinion of an independent scientist about whether use of a chainsaw is necessary to acquire adequate samples. Such frank and back-and-forth discussion is critical to minimizing impacts while still allowing data to be collected that is sufficient to fulfill the purposes of the research.

One of the purposes of this Quality of Proposal Filter is to promote up-front discussion between management staff and scientists. Requiring discussion of benefits and impacts in the proposal should encourage scientists to discuss their ideas with management staff *before* the proposal is submitted. While initially time consuming, such discussion should lead to a proposal that provides more useful information to managers, maximizes benefits, minimizes impacts, and fosters a more productive and mutually beneficial relationship between managers and scientists.

Legal and Policy Filter

This Filter (fig. 2) evaluates conformance of the proposal with existing legislation and applicable agency policies. In essence, proposed activities that violate existing law (the Wilderness Act and other Federal laws) or agency policy are not allowed in wilderness or other public lands. In practice, however, determining legislative and policy conformance is complex because of the way different laws overlap and how they interact with policies and other administrative direction—therefore, evaluating conformance may require subjective judgments. These judgments may pose less of a problem if any underlying assumptions and rationale are made explicit. As discussed above, this Legal and Policy Filter does not replace or fulfill NEPA or other compliance requirements. Each agency has distinct policy direction on research and other science activities inside wilderness, and staff members must defer to their agency's policies over this evaluation framework. Agency policies on research, as of the time this evaluation framework was published, are given in Appendix C.

The first step in this filter is to determine whether a proposal includes a use or activity that is generally prohibited by Section 4(c) of the Wilderness Act of 1964. The Act lists several uses and activities that are generally prohibited, including erecting structures and installations and using non-motorized mechanical transport, motor vehicles, motorized equipment, motorboats, and

USDA Forest Service Gen. Tech. Rep. RMRS-GTR-234WWW. 2010

10

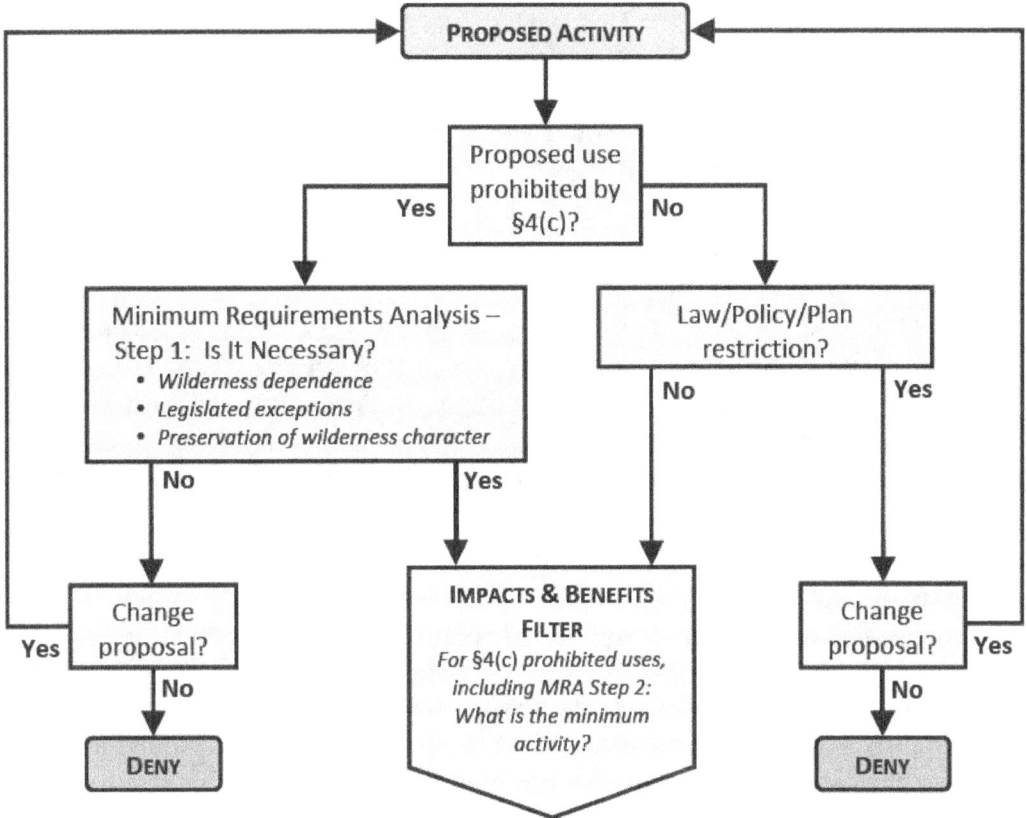

Figure 2—Legal and Policy Filter

landing aircraft (dropping or picking things up from aircraft that do not land is managed by regulation or policy specific to each agency). In a well-written proposal, this decision point is simple because it will be clearly stated whether one of these uses is proposed.

However, the prohibition of these uses is not absolute. If one of the uses is proposed, the manager must determine whether it meets the 1964 Wilderness Act Section 4(c) exemption of being "necessary to meet minimum requirements for the administration of the area for the purpose of [the Wilderness] Act." This statement has been the source of much debate because it is unclear exactly what is meant by "necessary," "minimum," and "administration." Different agencies, different offices within an agency, and different people all may use different definitions and criteria for determining which activities may be permitted under Section 4(c). Anderson (1999) offers a detailed discussion of this Section 4(c) phrase and its implication for research activities in wilderness. It is not the purpose of this evaluation framework to resolve these debates; however, anyone conducting an impact assessment must be aware of this uncertainty as a source of reasonable disagreement and contention. In such cases, agency staff must carefully document the rationale and any underlying assumptions used to support this judgment.

In addition, science activities related to health and safety concerns may vacate the Section 4(c) prohibitions. For example, seismographs were installed in the Yosemite Wilderness to study whether precursor ground movement could predict rockfalls that would endanger visitors in the non-wilderness portion of Yosemite National Park. In this case, upfront discussion between the scientists and management staff resulted in a scaled-down version of the study that allowed the scientists to derive meaningful data while minimizing impacts to wilderness character.

It is important to note that assessing whether a proposed activity is prohibited by Section 4(c) is not the only screen in this Legal and Policy Filter, it is merely the most convenient starting point because of the higher burden of "necessity" placed on these prohibited activities by the Wilderness Act. The Wilderness Act also mandates that managers "preserve wilderness character," and evaluation of this critical mandate is made at several points in this Filter and throughout this evaluation framework.

Proposals with Section 4(c) Prohibited Uses

If an activity or use is proposed that is prohibited by Section 4(c), then a Minimum Requirements Analysis (MRA) is required to determine if the activity meets the "necessary to meet the minimum requirements" clause of the Wilderness Act. Different agencies have different procedures for conducting this MRA, but in this evaluation framework we use the Minimum Requirements Decision Guide (MRDG, available at http://www.wilderness.net), developed by the Arthur Carhart National Wilderness Training Center, as a general model. The first step in this analysis considers whether *any* scientific activity is necessary regardless of methodology. There are at least three questions that need to be answered to determine necessity: (1) Is the activity wilderness-dependent—that is, can it be conducted only inside wilderness and in no other place to provide the same benefits? (2) Are there provisions in other legislation that allow this activity? (3) Is the activity necessary to preserve wilderness character? One must recognize that whether a proposal passes these questions is to some extent a matter of opinion, and careful documentation of how the answers are reached is necessary.

Wilderness Dependence—One of the first questions the manager needs to ask is whether the scientific activity is wilderness-dependent. There are essentially two ways of looking at wilderness dependence:

- Is the scientific activity dependent on being conducted inside a wilderness, regardless of its particular location? For example, a researcher wants to study the personal therapeutic benefits of a wilderness experience and wants to interview people while they are inside the wilderness; in this case the research must be conducted inside a wilderness, although it doesn't matter which wilderness or even the exact location within a wilderness.

- Is the scientific activity dependent on being conducted at a particular location that just happens to be within wilderness? For example, a researcher wants to study a particular geological occurrence by installing a series of seismographs, and this site occurs only inside a designated wilderness; in this case, the designation of wilderness is incidental to the purpose of the research, although it can only be conducted within the wilderness.

A "yes" answer to either question generally supports permitting the scientific activity. However, as discussed in detail below, wilderness dependence does not guarantee that the proposed activity will be permitted because the full range of impacts and benefits still needs to be evaluated.

In some cases, a scientific proposal might be wilderness-dependent, but the results of the study will not be of immediate benefit to the preservation of wilderness character or management of the area. For example, there could be a need for a monitoring installation in wilderness that would be vital to help determine the effects of climate change and, therefore, greatly benefit society, but no other location is suitable. The installation is a Section 4(c) prohibited use, and every attempt must be made to either avoid locating the facility in wilderness or to collect the data without an installation. Factors such as cost, efficiency, and time constraints based on non-wilderness factors should not be used as criteria for excluding alternate methods and locations. The installation may be permitted if the monitoring station is the only possible method, and it must be placed in wilderness to make use of an undisturbed landscape or geophysical location that is available only in wilderness. While this type of monitoring could be considered part of the scientific value and a public purpose of wilderness (see the Preservation of Wilderness Character section below), the installation must pass through both the entire Minimum Requirements Analysis process and the Impacts and Benefits Filter to determine need and to justify approval.

A "no" answer to either question about wilderness dependence means that the proposal to conduct the research inside the wilderness fails to meet the legal minimum necessary requirement and must be denied. The researcher would have the opportunity to either move the research location outside wilderness or eliminate the prohibited use. As an example, a paleontologist proposes to use a backhoe—a prohibited use under Section 4(c)—inside wilderness to sample two tons of sediment from a particular geologic stratum and then screen the sediment for microfossils. The stratum extends outside the wilderness. If the scientist refuses to "give up" the prohibited tool, the research request must be denied as it can be satisfied outside the wilderness. Conversely, the scientist could give up the prohibited use and change the proposal to excavate using hand tools.

There may be situations where research requires a prohibited use and can be conducted outside the wilderness, but because of substantial benefits to preserving wilderness character the research may be permitted (or may even be desired) inside wilderness. For example, researchers can determine the occurrence and demography of grizzly bears, but this requires installations that are conspicuous—each covers an area of several square meters—and they must be left in place for several years (Kendall and others 2009). In this case, even though the installation is a prohibited use, the benefits of knowing about bear populations inside wilderness—as a component of the natural quality of wilderness character as well as for managing visitor use to avoid bear encounters—may outweigh the impacts of the research.

None of the above is intended to discourage wilderness-dependent research or research that does not require a prohibited use. In fact, mangers may encourage research in wilderness as long as it does not degrade wilderness character.

Legislated Exceptions—Another question in the Minimum Requirements Analysis is whether there is a legislative exception that would allow this generally prohibited activity. No law takes precedence over another unless it explicitly states that it does, leading to what may be difficult choices and tradeoffs as mangers seek to comply with all the laws that apply to an area. Managers must comply with the mandates of all the laws that affect the wilderness for which they are responsible, and in some cases, this other legislation may allow activities that are prohibited under the 1964 Wilderness Act. For example, while the use of motor vehicles and structures is generally prohibited inside wilderness, the Alaska National Interest Lands Conservation Act (Public Law 96-487) allows a variety of these uses. Similarly, the Wyoming Wilderness Act (Public Law 98-550, Section 201(a)11) allows "occasional motorized access" for the purpose of managing bighorn sheep in the Fitzpatrick Wilderness. Other non-wilderness legislation such as the Endangered Species Act of 1973 may impose additional exceptions to the general prohibitions of the Wilderness Act.

In some cases this Legal and Policy Filter may lead to questions about the meaning of specific sections or words in Congressional legislation. For example, there may be uncertainty about the meaning of "may" or "shall" when used in legislated special provisions, but this uncertainty can usually be resolved by referring to a standard legal text such as Garner (2001). In this case, the word "may" in legislation means that the agency has the discretion to consider a prohibited use, not that it must be approved. In effect "may" means that a prohibited use "may" or "may not" be permitted. In contrast, the word "shall" in legislation means that the prohibited use must be approved—but unless detailed specifications are given in the legislation, the wilderness managing agency has the authority to specify when, where, and how this use will occur.

As an example, the California Desert Protection Act of 1994 includes the special provision that "management activities to maintain or restore fish and wildlife populations...*may* be carried out...and *shall* include the use of motorized vehicles by the appropriate State agencies" (Public Law 103-433, Section 103(f), emphases added). To clarify interpretation of "may" and "shall" in this legislation, the Bureau of Land Management developed a series of policy documents to avoid uncertainty in the field about how to implement this provision (Watson and Brink 1996). In cases of ambiguous or uncertain legislative direction, Federal and State personnel can refer to the appropriate legislative history and judicial decisions to help understand the intent of Congress (Meyer 1999), although this type of information is also open to interpretation.

Preservation of Wilderness Character—Before determining whether any activity should be undertaken (the MRA Step 1 decision), the manager also needs to determine if it is necessary to "preserve wilderness character," which is the primary wilderness stewardship mandate from Congress.

Congressional intent for the meaning of wilderness character is expressed in the Definition of Wilderness, Section 2(c) of the 1964 Wilderness Act (McCloskey 1999; Rohlf and Honnold 1988; Scott 2002). Recent agency reports (Landres and others 2005; Landres and others 2008) use this legal definition to identify four tangible and equally important qualities of wilderness character:

- *Untrammeled*—Wilderness is essentially unhindered and free from modern human control or manipulation.
- *Natural*—Wilderness ecological systems are substantially free from the effects of modern civilization.
- *Undeveloped*—Wilderness retains its primeval character and influence and is essentially without permanent improvement or modern human occupation.
- *Solitude or a primitive and unconfined type of recreation*—Wilderness provides outstanding opportunities for solitude or primitive and unconfined recreation.

In addition to these four qualities of wilderness character that legally apply to every wilderness, the Section 2(c) Definition of Wilderness states that a wilderness "may also contain ecological, geological, or other features of scientific, educational, scenic, or historical value." In other words, every wilderness may have "features" that are part of the wilderness character of the area but not represented in one of the four qualities described above. A key part of this sentence is the word "may" because some wildernesses may have such features while other areas do not—where they do occur, these features are a unique part of the area's wilderness character.

Features that are ecological or geological would typically be considered part of the natural quality of wilderness character. Examples of these could include species (e.g., threatened, endangered, endemic, or of other scientific interest such as thermophilic bacteria), unique geological formations (e.g., instrusive plutons), or paleontological resources (e.g., fossils). Other features could include cultural and historical sites that are protected under the Archaeological Resources Protection Act, Native American Graves Protection and Repatriation Act, and the National Historic Preservation Act.

In addition, the idea of wilderness character is broader than the tangible, legal qualities of wilderness character and other site-specific features that may occur within a wilderness. There are also intangible values associated with a wilderness. For example, spiritual, existence, or bequest values of wilderness may not be bound to the physical existence of an area and have little or nothing to do with its management. These values, though intangible, are still part of wilderness character and appropriate for scientific study.

Ultimately, the manager needs to determine whether the purpose of the proposed scientific activity is necessary to preserve wilderness character. This determination may often require subjective judgment that balances the impacts of the activity with its benefits, and careful documentation is needed.

In rare cases, preserving the scientific value of a unique feature may degrade one or more of the other qualities of wilderness character. Barns (2000), for example, described how the use of a helicopter was considered appropriate and the minimum necessary tool to remove a large and rare fossil from the wilderness before erosion destroyed it (fig. 3a). The use of a helicopter clearly temporarily degrades the undeveloped quality of the wilderness and the quality of solitude or primitive and unconfined recreation. Removal of the fossil is also a minor—though nonetheless real—degradation of the natural quality. But the fossil's removal was essential to preserve a unique value: the scientific knowledge of the species that millions of years ago inhabited what is now wilderness, which, without action, would have been lost to erosion.

Figure 3—(A) A helicopter was considered the minimum necessary tool to remove an intact rare fossil from the Bisti/De-Na-Zin Wilderness in New Mexico. (B) The use of hand tools was required to excavate this fossil. Photos by Chis Barns.

Analyzing this kind of tradeoff—where a scientific activity would degrade one aspect of wilderness character to preserve another—certainly poses a dilemma and different people could reasonably come to different conclusions about whether to allow such action. All such decisions require upfront and explicit communication between scientists and managers and careful documentation.

Making the "Step 1" Decision—After addressing these screens of the MRA, a decision must be made whether *any* action is "necessary to meet minimum requirements for the administration of the area for the purpose of [the Wilderness] Act," that is, to preserve wilderness character. If the activity is deemed to not fulfill this requirement, the proposal should be returned with suitable explanation and the opportunity should be given to amend the proposal by excluding the prohibited activity, bolstering how the activity would preserve wilderness character, or both.

If this decision is that some action is necessary, then it must be determined whether the proposed activity is the *minimum* necessary, fulfilling Step 2 of the MRA. The Impacts and Benefits Filter can be used to determine whether the proposed activity fulfills this legal requirement. (Determining the "minimum necessary" is part of the legal requirement and, therefore, could have been included in the Legal and Policy Filter; instead we include it in the Impacts and Benefits Filter so the tools described there can be used to make and document this determination.) This determination requires developing a series of alternatives and then choosing the one that best meets this "minimum necessary" legal requirement. The minimum necessary may or may not be the activity from the original proposal. Furthermore, the various component steps in a proposal may each be assigned different determinations on what the minimum necessary is. For example, in the fossil excavation and removal example described above, no motorized equipment was permitted for the excavation (hand tools were used; fig. 3b) and helicopter use to remove the fossil was limited to one day (Barns 2000). Determining this minimum will most likely not be a linear process, but instead require extensive discussion between the manager and scientist to derive a compromise that minimizes impacts to wilderness character while allowing the necessary scientific activity.

Proposals Without Section 4(c) Prohibited Uses

If no use or activity that is generally prohibited by Section 4(c) of the 1964 Wilderness Act is planned (either in the original proposal or after it was revised following the MRA process previously described), the proposal is reviewed to see if it is affected by some other legal, policy, or plan restriction. For example, researchers may propose collecting data in a particular area but the management plan severely restricts the number of people allowed in that area. If there is a restriction, then the proponent has the opportunity to amend the proposal to avoid the restriction. If there is no restriction the proposal moves on to the Impacts and Benefits Filter.

It is possible that a proposal does not involve a use prohibited by Section 4(c) but clearly degrades wilderness character and would thereby be denied. For example, a proposal to study the effects of predator removal (by hunting but with none of the prohibited uses) on the natural distribution and abundance of prey would clearly degrade the natural quality of wilderness character. However, such situations would likely be caught in the Initial Review Filter and the proposal would be returned before any further evaluation. In circumstances that are less clear but still dubious, these concerns will be caught by the Impacts and Benefits Filter.

Wilderness dependence may also be a consideration even though there are no Section 4(c) prohibited uses. In practice, even without Section 4(c) prohibited uses, proposals for science activities will range from having no impact other than the presence of the researcher to having substantial impact. For example, a proposal to measure the stand structure and diameter of trees inside a wilderness has very little impact, and the managers may gain new information about the area. In contrast, a proposal to collect specimens or to intensely manipulate or disturb an area using hand tools nonetheless has a significant impact. In this latter case, wilderness dependence should be considered in evaluating the proposal.

If a proposal has no Section 4(c) prohibited uses, different agency policies require different types of actions. For example, National Park Service policy requires an MRA for all administrative actions inside wilderness, including approving scientific activities, whereas the other agencies do not require this analysis. Forest Service policy requires evaluating wilderness dependence for all proposed scientific activities regardless of whether there is a prohibited use or not, whereas the other agencies do not.

Impacts and Benefits Filter

The purpose of the Impacts and Benefits Filter is to comprehensively and systematically assess the potential impacts and benefits of a proposed activity. Traditionally, evaluation processes review only the legal and policy aspects of a proposal, or only the impacts, or they ask only whether the proposed study must be conducted inside wilderness (see Landres and others 2003 for discussion about why these are necessary but insufficient). This Impacts and Benefits Filter takes a very different approach by acknowledging the complexity of scientific project proposals and the uncertainty of many decisions involving the "minimum necessary" mandate of the Wilderness Act for Section 4(c) prohibited uses. This Filter explicitly asks whether the impacts necessary to achieve the benefits are acceptable. This new approach acknowledges that every management action compromises or diminishes some aspect of wilderness character, but certain actions may still be allowed because an implicit tradeoff has been made in which the benefits outweigh the impacts. For example, bridges, trails, and toilets are installed for resource protection, yet they diminish other aspects of wilderness character. This approach is certainly different philosophically and practically from traditional approaches used to evaluate proposals for scientific activities, and it better represents the reality of making difficult decisions.

For proposals that include activities with a Section 4(c) prohibited use that were deemed by the Legal and Policy Filter to be "necessary," the Impacts and Benefits Filter is used to complete Step 2 of the MRA to determine what types of activity are the "minimum." The legal requirement from the Wilderness Act is that Section 4(c) prohibited uses may be permitted only if they are the "minimum necessary." Using these two filters in combination allows agency staff to first evaluate whether the activities are necessary, and then determine what the minimum activities are. To fulfill MRA Step 2, several alternatives to the activity from the proposal need to be identified and run through the Impacts and Benefits Filter. The activity with the smallest impact would be considered the minimum. However, some alternatives will also diminish the benefits of the proposal, and this Filter should also show any tradeoffs between impacts and benefits from the different alternatives.

This Impacts and Benefits Filter is composed of several steps (fig. 4). Basically, a proposal is run through a benefits assessment and an impacts assessment, yielding a numerical score for each. This score is then categorized or rated as either "low," "medium," or "high" benefit, and "low," "medium," or "high" impact. These resulting categories are then weighed against one another in a table that yields a provisional recommendation about whether to accept or deny the proposal.

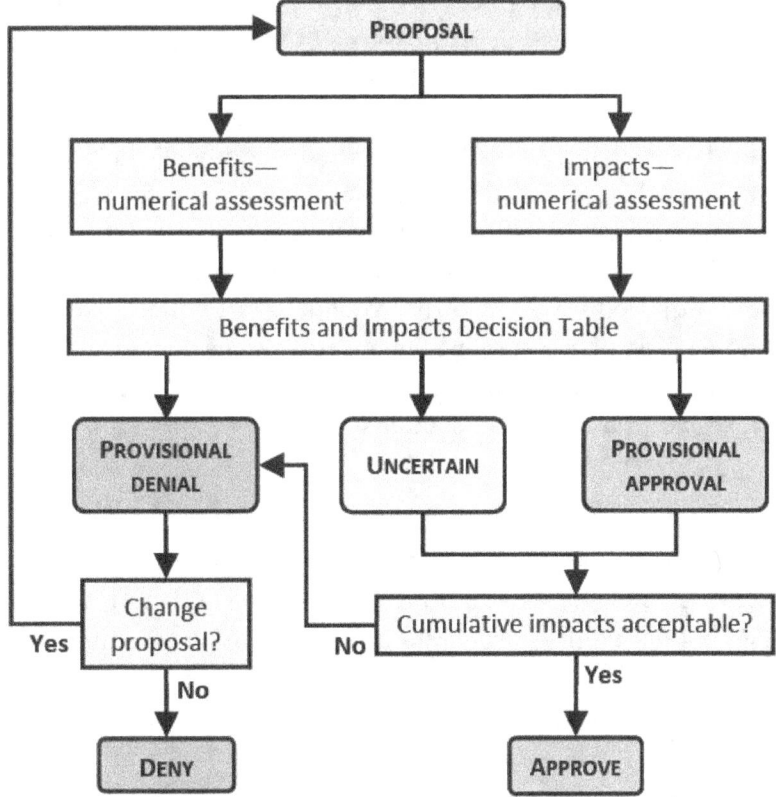

Figure 4—Impacts and Benefits Filter.

Numerical Scoring

This filter uses numerical scores to assess benefits and impacts. The advantages of using numerical scores include:

- making explicit the thought processes and subjective judgments management staff members use in weighing benefits and impacts, in turn providing a strong basis for discussion between management staff and scientists; and
- tallying numerical scores to assess cumulative impacts (1) within a single proposal from an accumulation of relatively small impacts, and (2) across all scientific activities, across larger areas, and across longer time frames.

The use of numerical scores in assessing benefits and impacts, however, creates a potential problem because of the tendency to assume that the scores have meaning and value, when in fact *the numerical scores have no inherent meaning or value*. For example, in the assessment of benefits, a proposal that is of limited use to management would receive a score of "2" while a proposal that is specifically designed to address a stewardship issue would receive a score of "10." The 2 and 10 have no inherent meaning or value—the 10 does not represent a 5-fold increase over the 2. Rather, these numbers merely represent the collective opinion of staff about the relative magnitude of benefit.

Local Flexibility

Local flexibility in assessing benefits and impacts *requires* local staffs to make several judgments. Although this creates an added work burden, the ecological, social, administrative, and legal context of a specific area already requires local staffs to be engaged in making a variety of professional judgments. Typically, local staffs would make these judgments just once before any proposal is evaluated and then use those judgments for evaluating all future proposals. This evaluation framework makes these local judgments transparent, allowing scientists to see exactly how local staffs weigh certain aspects of the proposed work, in turn providing for explicit discussion and better communication between management staff and scientists.

Local judgments are required for several aspects of this Impacts and Benefits Filter (as explained in the relevant sections below):

- Benefits Assessment
  - Identifying the categories of management and scientific benefits that will be used for scoring in the Benefits Assessment Worksheet
  - Assigning a numerical weighting factor for each benefit category
  - Assigning cut-points to separate categories of low, medium, and high benefit

- Impacts Assessment
  - Identifying the types of impacts and the numerical scoring that will be used in the Impacts Assessment Worksheet

- Developing documentation for the rationale used in assigning these numerical scores
- Assigning cut-points to separate categories of low, medium, and high impact

- Benefits and Impacts Decision Table
  - Assigning the outcomes (provisional approval, uncertain, provisional denial) for each cell of the table

- Cumulative Impacts Assessment
  - Identifying the types of cumulative impacts that may occur and their effect on the final decision about a proposal

Depending on the type of science activity proposed, the type of resources, and the complexity and potential problems of the proposal, a variety of inter-disciplinary management staff may need to be involved to ensure fair and balanced judgments in developing the worksheets and evaluating a proposal.

There will always be tension between standardized processes and local and situational flexibility; this framework strives to provide appropriate and necessary flexibility without rendering meaningless the benefits of using a standardized process. Nevertheless, local offices may abuse this flexibility to accommodate a specific proposal or person, thereby defeating the purpose of this evaluation framework. An agency may recommend certain limits to local flexibility to constrain this potential for abuse.

Benefits Assessment

Scientific activities may provide knowledge to help improve wilderness stewardship, that is, knowledge that helps preserve wilderness character within a specific wilderness or elsewhere across the National Wilderness Preservation System. Scientific activities to preserve wilderness character could benefit any of the four qualities of wilderness character (Landres and others 2008) as well as the unique features of an area described above in the Legal and Policy Filter:

- *Untrammeled*—for example, to understand the impacts of altering the frequency and effects of natural disturbances such as fire or flooding; or to understand the impacts of introducing non-indigenous species such as fish or livestock, or removing species such as indigenous predators.
- *Natural*—for example, to inventory and monitor the distribution of non-indigenous invasive plants; to restore the effects of natural fire regimes; to understand the effects of structures such as dams on native plants and animals; to monitor air pollutants and their effects; to understand geological features; or to monitor and understand the effects of global climate change.

- *Undeveloped*—for example, to understand how to naturalize or restore areas that have been degraded (such as campsites, trails, or areas around administrative structures); how to remove structures without using motorized equipment and mechanical transport; and how to efficiently inventory and monitor unauthorized developments.

- *Solitude or a primitive and unconfined type of recreation*—for example, to understand the impacts of management actions (such as use of permits, designated campsites, or agency-provided structures, such as bear poles or bear boxes, to protect campers' food from wildlife) on visitor experiences; to understand and monitor the things that affect solitude; and to understand the role of night sky visibility on visitor experiences.

- *Unique features*—for example, to understand how to best preserve a unique type of cultural site, or to understand the contribution of historical sites inside the wilderness to patterns of settlement throughout the broader region.

Scientific activities to help improve wilderness stewardship could provide knowledge about:

- *Urgent or important stewardship issues*—for example, to understand the impacts of shifting patterns of use (such as from more dispersed overnight use to more concentrated day use) on the occurrence of a rare plant and on visitor perceptions of solitude. Management may be considering imposing restrictions on the use of certain areas to mitigate adverse effects on the rare plant and on solitude, and there is an urgent need for baseline information on current conditions from which to assess impacts of management action. There may also be an urgent need for research that develops an early warning about how wilderness character is degrading in order to avoid problems before they require more drastic action.

- *Evaluating the effectiveness of past management decisions or actions*—for example, to understand how to most efficiently restore degraded campsites and trails; or to evaluate the impact of using designated campsites on visitor perceptions of primitive and unconfined recreation; or to understand the impacts of installing developed water sources for certain species on the other species that occur in the wilderness.

Last, the benefits from scientific activities for wilderness stewardship need to be evaluated in terms of how the results could be applied:

- *Immediately or in the future*—research designed to provide immediate results may be of greater benefit than research designed to offer results only after 20 years of study. For example, research showing current patterns of day use and overnight use, and their impacts, would likely be of more immediate benefit to managers compared to a study proposing to understand how visitor perceptions will change over the coming years.

- *As tangible management action*—research designed to give managers information that can result in on-the-ground management may be of greater benefit than research that cannot be acted on. For example, research on whether the use of designated campsites has actually reduced impacts to soil and vegetation or reduced user encounters can result in tangible action—continuing to require the use of designated camping or stopping this practice. Conversely, research on the contribution of night sky visibility to visitor's experience may be important but does not result in information managers can use if the primary source of light pollution is a nearby city.

- *Locally or only broadly*—research designed to help preserve wilderness character within a specific wilderness may be of greater benefit than research designed across many areas that may be only generally applicable to any individual area. For example, intensive research with multiple sites on snowpack trends may show the direct impact of global climate change within a wilderness, whereas research designed to show broad, region-wide trends with just one or two snowpack sites per wilderness may not yield information beneficial to the local wilderness.

Benefits to science may be applicable to specific fields of study or more broadly to knowledge in general. People proposing the scientific activity are responsible for describing and justifying science benefits; if these benefits are not sufficiently justified, the manager has the responsibility to ask for help from appropriate resource staff to review these benefits. Like management benefits, benefits to science are divided into several different categories:

- How geographically broad will the benefits to science be? For example, would the results improve understanding about a phenomenon that occurs only in a portion of the wilderness, across the entire wilderness, in every wilderness, or across an entire region?

- How far over time will the results benefit science? For example, would the results provide understanding that is short-term, such as one year, or long-term, such as the foreseeable future?

- How many different people or types of people will benefit from the results? For example, would the results benefit scientists in only one relatively narrow field of study; or would they benefit scientists in many different fields; or would they broadly benefit scientists and managers?

- How important is the activity to the scientific field of study? For example, would the results add a small increment of knowledge to a field of study, or would they be crucial to substantially advancing the discipline?

- What is the breadth of scientific inquiry? For example, would the results be applicable to a narrow field of study such as the taxonomy of a genus of beetles, or to many different fields of study such as the effect of climate change on vegetation, disturbance regimes, and wildlife habitat suitability?

Numerical Scoring of Benefits—A simple worksheet is used to numerically score benefits and derive a total benefits assessment score. A hypothetical example illustrating use of this worksheet is given in Appendix D and blank worksheets that staff can use for their own evaluation are given in Appendix E.

Within each of the benefit categories discussed above there is a range of possible benefits, and these are numerically scored from 0 to 10, with 0 having no benefit and 10 having the most. For each benefit category, an individual proposal may fall anywhere within this range. For example, a scientific study that directly addresses an important and urgent management issue would be rated a 10 for the benefit category focused on urgency, while a study that does not address an urgent management issue would be rated a 0.

The scores from each benefit category are then multiplied by a weighting factor. This weighting factor reflects local management staff perceptions about the relative importance of the benefit categories (see Appendix D for the rationale used in the hypothetical example worksheet). This relative importance is based on a combination of factors, including legislative direction, planning guidance, ecological and social context for the area, agency and local office culture, as well as association with scientists (e.g., an affiliation with a local science center). Discussion between agency staff and scientists could help inform these weighting decisions and create more open channels for communication. For computational ease, the weights across the 11 benefit categories add to 10, so each category is assigned a weight that is a fraction of 10. When the weighted scores for all benefit categories are added together, the total benefits assessment score can range from 0 (no benefit) to 100 points (maximum benefit).

This total score is then assigned a summary rating of low, medium, or high benefit. Local staffs previously determine the numerical cut-points that separate these three ratings such as 0 to 25, 26 to 75, and 76 to 100. Local staffs may feel that using only three summary benefits ratings does not provide sufficient ability to evaluate proposals, so they may choose instead to use four categories of benefit such as low, moderate, moderately high, and high.

Impacts Assessment

Traditionally, evaluating proposals for scientific activities in wilderness focused almost exclusively on impacts. Assessing impacts is critically important in this framework, but it is part of a more comprehensive evaluation that also takes into account the benefits of the proposed activity.

Nearly all modern human activities cause impacts to wilderness, yet acceptability of the impact varies from one activity to another, from one situation to the next, and from one person to another, often with little consistency or adequate definition. Acceptability can also change over time. For example, relatively pristine wilderness conditions are increasingly unique, and scientists may feel that certain ecological and social science research within wilderness yields benefits of increasingly greater value beyond the boundaries of the wilderness. In contrast, managers may feel that protecting the wilderness values of these same places is likewise increasingly important, including protection from the impacts of scientific activities that provide only broad-scale and more loosely defined or merely potential societal benefits.

Some agency policies direct managers to consider wilderness values foremost in deciding what types of activities are appropriate. For example, Forest Service Manual direction (Section 2320.6) states, "where a choice must be made between wilderness values...or any other activity, *preserving the wilderness resource is the overriding value*. Economy, convenience, commercial value, and comfort are not standards of management or use of wilderness" (emphasis added). The National Park Service has similar policy language. Under such policies, it is appropriate for management staff to question all scientific activities that may adversely affect wilderness character and the ecological or social values of wilderness, and to place wilderness values over and above other values. For example, the installation of a battery, solar panels, and an antenna to provide real-time information to a scientist must help preserve wilderness character and not be merely for the convenience of the scientist. This question about unacceptable impacts should lead to explicit discussion about the methods that are appropriate and acceptable in wilderness to accomplish the objectives of the proposed activity.

Statutory Classification of Impacts—To tie this impacts assessment directly to the statutory language of the 1964 Wilderness Act, impacts are categorized by the four qualities of wilderness character (Landres and others 2005), as follows:

- Untrammeled
    - Manipulation (includes introducing, restoring, removing [e.g., to study what's left behind], moving, or disturbing [e.g., wildlife collaring, trapping, feeding, sampling, coring trees] any aspect of the "community of life")

- Natural
    - Collecting (biophysical, geological, or anthropological items)

- Undeveloped
    - Mechanical transport
    - Motorized equipment
    - Installations and structures

- Solitude or a primitive and unconfined type of recreation
    - Group size
    - Total person-days per season
    - Visitor surveys
    - Surveillance

This categorization scheme allows assessing the impact from a single activity (such as one installation), multiple activities (such as several installations), different types of activities (such as installations and the use of motorized equipment), and cumulatively across administrative and scientific activities on each quality of wilderness character. Placing the impacts from a proposed activity in this statutory context allows management staff to understand how the proposed activity affects their legal responsibility to preserve wilderness character. It may also help address the tradeoffs when there is a benefit to one or more quality of wilderness character but adverse effects on others. Other types of concerns such as how the proposed work might affect safety or park operations are not considered in this evaluation framework but may enter into the final decision.

Numerical Scoring of Impacts—A simple worksheet is used to numerically score impacts and derive a total impacts assessment score. A hypothetical example illustrating use of this worksheet and the rationale behind the impact scoring is given in Appendix D and blank worksheets that staff can use for their own evaluation are given in Appendix E. Local staffs will need to develop an Impacts Assessment Worksheet that shows the impact categories (or types of impacts), variation in the magnitude or intensity within each type of impact, and the numerical scores that would be assigned to the different types of activities that could occur under each impact category. Activities or uses prohibited by Section 4(c) of the 1964 Wilderness Act would typically receive the highest numerical impact scores. Local staffs will need to make many decisions based on professional judgment to develop this Worksheet. Once completed, this Worksheet is the basis for evaluating impacts from proposed activities and will be a key tool in communicating and negotiating with scientists.

Scoring the Impacts Assessment Worksheet differs from the Benefits Assessment Worksheet in three ways. First, to allow impact scoring that can range from very small to very large, impact scores are divided more finely to allow a more precise level of evaluation at the low end of impact, and an additional "plus" column is added to accommodate large impacts. This "plus" column allows the manager to evaluate the few proposals that would have a truly high impact. Second, there is no separate weighting factor column because the degree of impact was built into how the scores would be assigned. Third, this is an open-ended scoring system with no maximum numerical limit.

Once the separate impacts assessments are completed they are summed to derive a total score. This total score is then assigned a summary rating of low, medium, or high impact. Local staffs previously determine the numerical cutpoints that separate these ratings. Local staffs may feel that using only three summary ratings of impact does not provide sufficient ability to evaluate proposals, so they may choose instead to use four impact ratings such as not detectible, low, medium, and high.

Benefits and Impacts Decision Table

The goal of the benefits and impacts decision table is to weigh impacts against benefits to determine whether the benefits are sufficient to outweigh the impacts (or stated differently, whether the impacts are acceptable to achieve the benefits). Local circumstances such as enabling legislation or other language used in the establishment of a wilderness that specifically addresses scientific and research uses of the wilderness may affect this weight or balance. For example, the 1925 Presidential Proclamation establishing Glacier Bay National Monument (and the area that was designated as Glacier Bay Wilderness in 1980) states, "this area presents a unique opportunity for the scientific study of glacial behavior and of resulting movements and development of flora and fauna and of certain valuable relics of ancient interglacial forests."

In the example table (table 1), local staffs decide where the entries "Provisional Approval," "Provisional Denial," and "Uncertain" are placed (the entries in this table are only for the purpose of illustrating how this table is used). "Provisional Approval" means that local staffs believe the benefits are sufficient to outweigh the impacts, and the proposal is provisionally accepted to move on to the next step. "Provisional Denial" means that local staffs believe the benefits are not sufficient to outweigh the impacts. In this case the proposal is provisionally denied and the scientists are given an opportunity to modify their proposal to reduce the impacts and increase the benefits. After the proposal has been revised, it will need to be reevaluated in the Impacts and Benefits Filter because both impacts and benefits may be different from what they were. "Uncertain" means that there is insufficient information to make a determination about the proposal and that further evaluation and discussion is needed among staff and between staff and the scientists.

Table 1—A hypothetical Benefits and Impacts Decision Table showing how local staff may assign the evaluations of "Provisional approval," "Provisional denial," or "Uncertain" based on the interplay between benefits and impacts.

		BENEFITS		
		Low	Medium	High
IMPACTS	Low	Provisional approval	Provisional approval	Provisional approval
	Medium	Provisional denial	Uncertain	Uncertain
	High	Provisional denial	Uncertain	Uncertain

Cumulative Impacts Assessment

For cases where the recommendation from the Benefits and Impacts Decision Table is either "Provisional Approval" or "Uncertain," managers should conduct an assessment of cumulative impacts. The purpose of this assessment is to place the proposed activity in the context of impacts from all the other activities occurring in the area (for example, from management and from other scientific as well as recreational activities) and ask whether the accumulated impacts from all these activities are acceptable. The concern is not with the impacts of the individual proposal being analyzed, but with how these impacts add to those from all the other activities that have occurred, are occurring, or will likely occur in the area. If the proposed activity adds the increment of impact that makes the total impact unacceptable, then the proposal may need to be modified to reduce its impacts or be denied. Therefore, the effect of the cumulative impacts assessment on the overall decision is either neutral, if there are minor or no cumulative impacts, or negative, if there are significant cumulative impacts.

Cumulative impacts are complex and typically not considered in assessing impacts of scientific activities. However, as wilderness becomes increasingly recognized for its role providing baseline or benchmark data, cumulative impacts are becoming more of a concern (Landres 2005). There are several different types of cumulative impact, including:

- Spatial
  - Assessed across the entire wilderness
  - Assessed within special areas within the wilderness
- Temporal
  - Each project is assessed within the context of all projects that are being conducted in the current year
  - Each project is assessed within the context of all projects that were started in previous years
  - Each project is assessed within the context of all projects that will likely be conducted in the future
- Effects of a particular type of impact regardless of source (for example, research and other scientific activities, management such as search and rescue or administrative use, and visitor use)
- Effects across all impact categories
- Impacts to the four qualities of wilderness character
- Impacts to selected resources (for example, selected species or ecological processes)

Cumulative impacts could be assessed using GIS or tabular databases, if such data exist. In addition, specific thresholds for triggering concern would need to be established by local staff (for example, the number of projects occurring within a particular area, or the number of people within a certain area). While a "hard" threshold that would cause a proposal to be rejected is possible, the complexity in assessing cumulative impacts suggests that this would be relatively rare. Far more likely would be a "yellow light" threshold that would trigger the need to negotiate to increase benefits (for example, for management applicability) or decrease impacts (for example, go to a different watershed, conduct the study at a different time of year or the following year, or remove research or other installations in the area that staff previously wanted gone), or both.

References

Albright, H.M. 1933. Research in the national parks. The Scientific Monthly 36:483-501.

Anderson, R.L. 1999. Research administration in wilderness: defining the "minimum requirement" exception. Pages 415-417 *in* On the Frontiers of Conservation: Proceedings of the 10th Conference on Research and Resource Management in Parks and on Public Lands (D. Harmon, editor). The George Wright Society, Hancock, MI.

Barns, C.V. 2000. Paleontological excavations in designated wilderness: theory and practice. Pages 155-159 *in* Wilderness Science in a Time of Change, Volume 3 (S.F. McCool, D.N. Cole, W.T. Borrie, J. O'Loughlin, compilers). USDA Forest Service Rocky Mountain Research Station Proceeding RMRS-P-15-VOL-3, Fort Collins, CO.

Bayless, J. 1999. Regulating National Park Service research and collecting: a fifty-year search for a legal, flexible, and standardized approach. Pages 418-422 *in* On the Frontiers of Conservation: Proceedings of the 10th Conference on Research and Resource Management in Parks and on Public Lands (D. Harmon, editor). The George Wright Society, Hancock, MI.

Bratton, S.P. 1988. Environmental monitoring in wilderness. Pages 103-112 *in* Wilderness Benchmark, Proceedings of the National Wilderness Colloquium. USDA Forest Service General Technical Report SE-51, Southeastern Forest Experiment Station, Asheville, NC.

Butler, L.M., and R.S. Roberts. 1986. Use of wilderness areas for research. Pages 398-405 *in* Proceedings—National Wilderness Research Conference: Current Research (R.C. Lucas, compiler). USDA Forest Service General Technical Report INT-212, Intermountain Research Station, Ogden, UT.

Eichelberger, J., and A. Sattler. 1994. Conflict of values necessitates public lands research policy. Transactions of the American Geophysical Union 75:505-508.

Franklin, J.F. 1987. Scientific use of wilderness. Pages 42-46 *in* Proceedings--National Wilderness Research Conference: Issues, State-of-Knowledge, Future Directions (R.C. Lucas, compiler). USDA Forest Service General Technical Report INT-220, Intermountain Research Station, Ogden, UT.

Garner, B.A. 2001. A Dictionary of Modern Legal Usage, 2nd Edition. Oxford University Press, New York, NY.

Graber, D.M. 1988. The role of research in wilderness. George Wright Forum 5(4):55-59

Graber, D.M. 2002. Scientific values of public parks. George Wright Forum 19(2):63-66.

Kendall, K.C., J. Boulanger, A.C. Macleod, D. Paetkau, and G.C. White. 2009. Demography and genetic structure of a recovering grizzly bear population. Journal of Wildlife Management 73:3-17.

Landres, P. 2005. Balancing the benefits and impacts of science in Alaska's wilderness. Alaska Park Science 4(2):44-46.

Landres, P., J. Alderson, and D.J. Parsons. 2003. The challenge of doing science in wilderness: historical, legal, and policy context. George Wright Forum 20(3):42-49.

Landres, P., S. Boutcher, L. Merigliano, C. Barns, D. Davis, T. Hall, S. Henry, B. Hunter, P. Janiga, M. Laker, A. McPherson, D.S. Powell, M. Rowan, and S. Sater. 2005. Monitoring selected conditions related to wilderness character: a national framework. USDA Forest Service Rocky Mountain Research Station General Technical Report RMRS-GTR-151, Fort Collins, CO.

Landres, P., C. Barns, J.G. Dennis, T. Devine, P. Geissler, C.S. McCasland, L. Merigliano, J. Seastrand, and R. Swain. 2008. Keeping it wild: an interagency strategy to monitor trends in wilderness character across the National Wilderness Preservation System. USDA Forest Service Rocky Mountain Research Station General Technical Report RMRS-GTR-212, Fort Collins, CO.

Leopold, A. 1949. A Sand County almanac and sketches here and there. Oxford University Press. London, England.

McCloskey, M. 1999. Changing views of what the wilderness system is all about. Denver University Law Review 76:369-381.

Meyer, S. 1999. The role of legislative history in agency decision making: a case study of wilderness airstrip management in the United States. International Journal of Wilderness 5(2):9-12.

USDA Forest Service Gen. Tech. Rep. RMRS-GTR-234WWW. 2010

29

Oelfke, J.G., R.O. Peterson, J.A. Vucetich, and L.M Vucetich. 2000. Wolf research in the Isle Royale Wilderness: do the ends justify the means? Pages 246-251 *in* Wilderness Science in a Time of Change, Volume 3 (S.F. McCool, D.N. Cole, W.T. Borrie, J. O'Loughlin, compilers). USDA Forest Service Rocky Mountain Research Station Proceeding RMRS-P-15-VOL-3, Fort Collins, CO.

Parsons, D.J. 2000. The challenge of scientific activities in wilderness. Pages 252-257 *in* Wilderness Science in a Time of Change, Volume 3 (S.F. McCool, D.N. Cole, W.T. Borrie, J. O'Loughlin, compilers). USDA Forest Service Rocky Mountain Research Station Proceeding RMRS-P-15-VOL-3, Fort Collins, CO.

Parsons, D.J., and D.M. Graber. 1991. Horses, helicopters and hi-tech: managing science in wilderness. Pages 90-94 *in* Preparing to Manage Wilderness in the 21st Century (P.C.

Public Law 88-577. Wilderness Act. September 3, 1964. 16 U.S.C. 1131-1136.

Public Law 96-487. Alaska National Interest Lands Conservation Act. December 2, 1980. 94 Statute 2371-2551.

Public Law 98-550. Wyoming Wilderness Act of 1984. October 30, 1984. 98 Statute 2807-2815.

Public Law 103-433. California Desert Protection Act of 1994. October 31, 1994. 108 Statute 4471-4525.

Reed, compiler). USDA Forest Service Southeastern Forest and Experiment Station General Technical Report SE-66, Asheville, NC.

Rohlf, D., and D.L. Honnold. 1988. Managing the balance of nature: the legal framework of wilderness management. Ecology Law Quarterly 15:249-279.

Peterson, D.L. 1996. Research in parks and protected areas: forging the link between science and management. Pages 417-434 *in* National Parks and Protected Areas: Their Role in Environmental Protection (R.G. Wright, J. Lemmons, editors). Blackwell Science.

Scott, D.W. 2002. "Untrammeled," "wilderness character," and the challenges of wilderness preservation. Wild Earth 11(3/4):72-79.

Sharman, L.C., P. Landres, and S. Boudreau. 2007. Developing a framework for evaluating proposals for research in wilderness: science to protect and learn from parks. Alaska Park Science 6(2):100-103.

Six, D.L., P. Alaback, R.A. Winfree, D. Snyder, and A. Hagele. 2000. Wilderness for science: pros and cons of using wilderness areas for biological research. Pages 271-275 *in* Wilderness Science in a Time of Change, Volume 3 (S.F. McCool, D.N. Cole, W.T. Borrie, J. O'Loughlin, compilers). USDA Forest Service Rocky Mountain Research Station Proceeding RMRS-P-15-VOL-3, Fort Collins, CO.

Stokstad, E. 2001. Utah's fossil trove beckons, and tests, researchers. Science 294:41-42.

Suarez, A.V. 2009. Science for parks/parks for science. Park Science 26(1):14-16.

Watson, J., and P. Brink. 1996. The California Desert Protection Act: a time for desert parks and wilderness. International Journal of Wilderness 2(2):14-17.

Zahniser, H. 1956. The need for wilderness areas. The Living Wilderness 59(Winter to Spring):37-43.

Appendix A—Hypothetical Example of Climate Change Research Evaluation

With the impacts of climate change becoming apparent, scientists from nearly every discipline are calling for more research. Should this research be conducted within designated wilderness? Many have suggested that wilderness would be an excellent place to conduct climate change research because wilderness is relatively unaffected by many of the direct anthropogenic environmental insults that occur in most other areas, so the signal of climate change and its effects may be clearer there than in other areas. Many wildernesses, because of their higher elevation or latitude, also present extreme climates that might serve as sentinels or an early warning of the effects from climate change. Others argue that since climate change research does not help the agencies preserve wilderness character, any impacts from such research are too great to justify and that there are plenty of areas outside wilderness that offer the same research opportunities. In a nutshell, climate change research epitomizes the acrimony that can develop among people with disparate viewpoints about research in wilderness. We developed this framework to help sort through these issues.

Our position is that there is nothing inherently incompatible about climate change research, or any research for that matter, being conducted inside wilderness. The importance and urgency of understanding the effects of climate change, however, does not exempt scientists from adhering to the legal requirements of the 1964 Wilderness Act. Many potential problems posed by climate change research can be avoided if scientists discuss their ideas and means for accomplishing the research with managers early in the proposal development process.

Assuming there are no red flags from the Initial Review Filter and the proposal is written well and passes the Quality of Proposal Filter, the major concern is whether the research requires a use or activity that is prohibited by Section 4(c) of the Wilderness Act. If no prohibited use or activity is proposed (for example, there are no installations and no use of motorized equipment), then the impacts and benefits of the research are evaluated in the Impacts and Benefits Filter and a decision is reached about whether to permit the work. Say, for example, field research will map the distribution of current treeline to observe how it changes over time to test climate model predictions across a variety of latitudes. This research has minimal impact from the researchers mapping treeline and provides clear benefits to science by improving the climate models. Such research would likely be permitted even though the presence of researchers would temporarily impact the solitude quality of wilderness character, and there is no immediate benefit to preserving wilderness character other than understanding the current distribution of treeline.

In contrast, if a Section 4(c) prohibited use or activity is proposed, the benefit bar will be raised in order for the research to be permitted. For example, researchers might want to install permanent data recorders to monitor water flow, temperature, precipitation, snowfall, or many others parameters that have importance for understanding the ecological effects of climate change. Or, researchers might want to use motorized equipment to drill and remove lake sediment cores to compare with climate model predictions about how the vegetation and disturbance regimes have changed over time in the area surrounding the lake. Both examples violate Section 4(c) and are, therefore, illegal unless they can be proven to meet the "minimum necessary" criteria discussed in the Legal and Policy Filter. These criteria are:

- the research is wilderness-dependent;
- the prohibited use or activity is the "minimum necessary;" and
- the research helps preserve wilderness character.

If scientists can document how their prohibited activities (installations and motorized equipment in this case) meet this legal requirement, the manager would next evaluate the proposed research in the Impacts and Benefits Filter to determine the "minimum necessary" to accomplish the research. In some cases, however, the research may meet the first two criteria but not the third or at least may not provide immediate benefit to preserving wilderness character. In such cases, we recommend moving forward to the Impacts and Benefits Filter to evaluate whether the benefits outweigh the impacts.

In every case where proposed research involves a Section 4(c) prohibited activity, because the immediate impacts to wilderness character are great, the benefits also need to be great in order for the research to be approved. The Impacts and Benefits Filter provides the opportunity for the manager and scientist to discuss specific requirements to minimize these impacts. These requirements, for example, might include camouflaging an installation in particular ways or suggesting other locations that would satisfy the research criteria but be less obvious to wilderness visitors. In some cases, these options to minimize impacts may also reduce the quality of the data, thereby reducing the potential benefits of the research. Such cases require close communication and cooperation between scientists and managers to discuss various options and their impacts and benefits. To avoid acrimony and hassle, the earlier this communication occurs, the better.

Resentment between climate scientists and wilderness managers would only add to the many tragedies caused by rapid climate change. Both groups share many values and goals centered on understanding and preserving the natural world. Climate scientists may feel that wilderness is the best place to conduct their research, while wilderness managers and advocates may feel that wilderness protection, precisely because of the pervasiveness of environmental threats and global climate change, should not be compromised. One purpose of this evaluation framework is to push both scientists and managers toward upfront communication and mutual understanding—doing so should decrease the impacts to wilderness character while allowing the wilderness to be used as a source of inspiration and scientific understanding.

Appendix B—Guidelines for Scientists Conducting Research in Wilderness

The following guidelines are for scientists who want to conduct scientific activities in wilderness. These are only brief guidelines intended to help scientists understand and communicate with local managers, thereby expediting the process of evaluating a proposal for scientific activities.

Education

Assure that you understand the special requirements for working in wilderness and why they exist.

1. Understand the legal requirements of the Wilderness Act and agency policy for conducting science activities inside wilderness. This includes understanding that the primary management responsibility is to preserve wilderness character. More information is available at http://www.wilderness.net.

2. Understand the legal prohibitions against using motorized equipment (such as drills), mechanical transport (such as game carts or any wheeled vehicles), landing aircraft, and installations (such as data loggers or plot markers), and under what conditions exceptions may be allowed.

3. Identify which local agency office(s) administer the portion(s) of the wilderness you want to work in. Be aware that some wildernesses are administered by more than one Federal agency.

4. Understand agency and local administrative procedures for evaluating your proposal and permit requirements for working in wilderness. Different local offices may have different requirements, and the four Federal agencies that administer wilderness have different policies for permitting scientific activities.

5. Ask yourself how your science will benefit the wilderness you would like to work in.

Communication

Communicate as early as possible with the local managers about what you want to do.

1. Make initial contact with the managers in *all* of the local offices that administer the portion(s) of the wilderness you are interested in working in. Do not assume that different offices communicate with one another or use the same procedures for evaluating a proposal for scientific activities.

2. Discuss your research interests and sampling design with the local managers *before* you write a proposal, and consult with them often as you develop your proposal.

3. Ask if there are any potential problems with any aspect of the research, including location, timing, access, number of people, type of equipment, type of work, monumentation, or purpose of the research. This discussion should center on how to minimize the impacts to wilderness character while still accomplishing your research objectives.

4. Ask if the local managers have any research or other needs that you could help with while you're in the backcountry. For example, a manager might ask you to report if you see a certain rare species or to remove unwanted debris from an area when your research crews come out of the wilderness.

5. Ask about local administrative and permitting requirements, and if needed, get a wilderness use and research permit. Try to establish contact with local managers before applying for funding. Do not assume that a permit will be granted simply because you already have funding, even if that funding is from the National Science Foundation or another prestigious source.

6. Ask the local managers if they would like you to prepare a small poster about your work that can be placed on the trailhead bulletin board to let wilderness visitors know what you are doing, as well as the general location of your research and when you will be there so visitors may avoid this area if they want to.

7. Ask the local managers how they would like to be informed when you are entering the wilderness, where you will be camped, and when you are leaving the wilderness.

8. Ask whether there are opportunities to present or share any aspect of your research with agency staff or visitors.

In the Field

You're working in a unique place that requires special skills, attitudes, and consideration of other wilderness visitors.

1. Make sure you and your crews have the gear and experience (or training) to work and live in wilderness.

2. Learn and practice "Leave No Trace" skills. Be aware that wilderness character is reduced by both ecological and social impacts. You can minimize these impacts by using equipment that is not brightly colored, avoiding areas the are frequently used by wilderness visitors, camping in areas that are remote or hidden, and generally being considerate of others who are there to enjoy solitude and primitive recreation.

3. Clean up and remove all evidence of your camping (such as fire rings and wood piled for fires) and your research (such as flagging, stakes, trash, and tags) to meet local requirements unless you are specifically permitted to leave certain items.

4. Be ready and willing to answer questions from any wilderness visitors you may encounter.

Appendix C—Agency Policies on Research and Scientific Activities

The following sections are taken directly from current agency policy regarding research and other scientific activities in wilderness. The policies given below are current as of the time this framework was published, but policies change over time and staff members must consult their own sources to ensure they are referencing the most current policy for their agency. In addition, only policies directly related to research and other scientific activities are included here, but other policies may also be relevant.

U.S Department of Agriculture—Forest Service

Forest Service wilderness policy is from the Forest Service Manual (FSM) 2300 Recreation, Wilderness, and Related Resource Management, Chapter 2320 Wilderness Management, as amended January 22, 2007.

2324.4—Research in Wilderness

2324.41—Objective. To provide appropriate opportunity for scientific studies that are dependent on a wilderness environment.

2324.42—Policy

1. Encourage research in wilderness that preserves the wilderness character of the area (FSM 2320.3).

2. Identify wilderness management or national issues that may require research in forest plans.

3. Review proposals to conduct research in wilderness to ensure that research areas outside wilderness could not provide similar research opportunities. Direct projects that would jeopardize wilderness values to areas outside wilderness.

4. Review research proposals to conduct research in wilderness to ensure that research methods are compatible with wilderness values. Do not allow the use of motorized equipment or mechanical transport unless the research is essential to meet minimum requirements for administration of the area as wilderness and cannot be done another way (Section 4(c) of the Wilderness Act). Include specific stipulations in the approval document.

5. Except for studies that clearly require contact within wilderness, allow interviews or direct contact with visitors only outside wilderness.
   6. Permit scientific study of cultural resource sites/areas consistent with the direction in FSM 2323.8.

U.S. Department of the Interior—Bureau of Land Management

Bureau of Land Management wilderness policy is from the Federal Register, Volume 65, Number 241, 78357-78376[00-31656]. Thursday, December 14, 2000.

43 CFR Part 6300—Management of Designated Wilderness Areas
Subpart 6302—Use of Wilderness Areas, Prohibited Acts, and Penalties

§ 6302.16—When and how may I gather scientific information about resources in BLM wilderness?

(a) You may conduct research, including gathering information and collecting natural or cultural resources in wilderness areas, using methods that may cause greater impacts on the wilderness environment than allowed under § 6302.15(a), if—

    (1) Similar research opportunities are not reasonably available outside wilderness;

    (2) You carry out your proposed activity in a manner compatible with the preservation of the wilderness environment and conforming to the applicable management plan;

    (3) Any ground disturbance or removal of material is the minimum necessary for the scientific purposes of the research; and

    (4) You have an authorization from BLM.

(b) You must reclaim disturbed areas, and BLM may require you to post a bond.

U.S. Department of the Interior—Fish and Wildlife Service

Fish and Wildlife Service wilderness policy is from its Natural and Cultural Resources Management, Part 610 Wilderness Stewardship, Chapter 2 Wilderness Administration and Resource Stewardship (610 FW2).

2.27 How does the Service conduct research in wilderness?

A. The scientific value of wilderness derives from the relatively undisturbed condition of the biophysical environment and its ecological and evolutionary processes. Because such undisturbed natural areas are increasingly rare, wilderness areas provide unique opportunities for scientific investigation. Everyone associated with research in wilderness must know and understand the purposes, values, and protective provisions of wilderness.

B. We will not allow or engage in research that has significant or long-term adverse impacts on wilderness character or refuge purposes.

C. We permit research in wilderness only if it furthers the administrative or educational objectives or scientific knowledge of the area. There must be a reasonable assurance that the benefits to be derived from the research outweigh any impacts on wilderness character. We require researchers to restore disturbed areas to their previous condition to the greatest extent practical. Existing and potential research activities should be described and evaluated in the refuge's WSP or CCP.

(1) Research as a Refuge Management Activity. We administer Refuge System and Refuge System sponsored research as refuge management activities. We will evaluate research proposals through an MRA (see 610 FW 1.18).

(2) Research as a Refuge Use. We may authorize private research in a wilderness area, with a special use permit (SUP) if it is appropriate and compatible with refuge purposes, including Wilderness Act purposes, and does not involve generally prohibited uses (see section 2.7 and 610 FW 1.16 for additional information).

2.28 How does the Service conduct inventory and monitoring activities in wilderness? Long-term wilderness stewardship requires that we inventory and monitor wilderness character. Conditions prevailing within a wilderness area at the time of designation serve as a benchmark for the area's wilderness character.

A. We will not allow degradation of these conditions.

B. We should conduct baseline inventories for key wilderness resources and identify the nature, magnitude, and source of any threats that originate both within and outside the wilderness area. Baseline data also provide a frame of reference for the limits, thresholds, and indicators identified in the WSP that may trigger refuge management activities, including limiting public use.

C. Inventories also give us the information necessary to evaluate the effects of refuge management activities, refuge uses, and external threats on wilderness character. We will evaluate proposed inventory and monitoring protocols and activities in an MRA and document inventory and monitoring activities in the refuge's WSP.

2.29 How does the Service protect cultural resources in wilderness?

B. Archeological Research. We administer archaeological research within wilderness areas according to the conditions outlined for research in section 2.27. We encourage archeological research employing noninvasive and nondestructive survey and inventory methods. The refuge manager and the RHPO will review proposals for archeological research. The Regional Director approves or denies archaeological research permits based on the recommendation of the refuge manager and Regional archeologist. We will approve archeological research requiring digging, trenching, or other forms of excavation in wilderness when required to protect a threatened resource. We may also approve other research involving excavation when it can be demonstrated that significant archaeological information may be obtained that cannot reasonably be expected to be obtained from nonwilderness lands.

USDA Forest Service Gen. Tech. Rep. RMRS-GTR-234WWW. 2010

37

U.S. Department of the Interior—National Park Service

National Park Service wilderness policy is from its 2006 Management Policies, Chapter 6: Wilderness Preservation and Management.

6.3.6 – Scientific Activities in Wilderness
The statutory purposes of wilderness include scientific activities, and these activities are encouraged and permitted when consistent with the Service's responsibilities to preserve and manage wilderness.

6.3.6.1 – General Policy
The National Park Service has a responsibility to support appropriate scientific activities in wilderness and to use science to improve wilderness management. The Service recognizes that wilderness can and should serve as an important resource for long-term research into and study and observation of ecological processes and the impact of humans on these ecosystems. The National Park Service further recognizes that appropriate scientific activities may be critical to the long-term preservation of wilderness.

Scientific activities are to be encouraged in wilderness. Even those scientific activities (including inventory, monitoring, and research) that involve a potential impact to wilderness resources or values (including access, ground disturbance, use of equipment, and animal welfare) should be allowed when the benefits of what can be learned outweigh the impacts on wilderness resources or values. However, all such activities must also be evaluated using the minimum requirement concept and include documented compliance that assesses impacts against benefits to wilderness. This process should ensure that the activity is appropriate and uses the minimum tool required to accomplish project objectives. Scientific activities involving prohibitions identified in section 4(c) of the Wilderness Act (16 USC 1133(c)) may be conducted within wilderness when the following occur:

- The desired information is essential for understanding the health, management, or administration of wilderness, and the project cannot be reasonably modified to eliminate or reduce the nonconforming wilderness use(s); or if it increases scientific knowledge, even when this serves no immediate wilderness management purposes, provided it does not compromise wilderness resources or character. The preservation of wilderness resources and character will be given significantly more weight than economic efficiency and/or convenience.

- Compliance with the National Environmental Policy Act (including completion of documented categorical exclusions, environmental assessments/ findings of no significant impact, or environmental impact statements/ records of decision) and other regulatory compliance (including compliance with section 106 of the National Historic Preservation Act (16 USC 470(f)) are accomplished and documented.

- All scientific activities will be accomplished in accordance with terms and conditions adopted at the time the research permit is approved. Later requests for exceptions to the Wilderness Act will require additional review and approval.
- The project will not significantly interfere with other wilderness purposes (recreational, scenic, educational, conservational, or historical) over a broad area or for a long period of time.
- The minimum requirement concept is applied to implementation of the project.

Research and monitoring devices (e.g., video cameras, data loggers, meteorological stations) may be installed and operated in wilderness if (1) the desired information is essential for the administration and preservation of wilderness and cannot be obtained from a location outside wilderness without significant loss of precision and applicability; and (2) the proposed device is the minimum requirement necessary to accomplish the research objective safely.

Park managers will work with researchers to make NPS wilderness area research a model for the use of low-impact, less intrusive techniques. New technology and techniques will be encouraged if they are less intrusive and cause less impact. The goal will be for studies in NPS wilderness to lead the way in "light on the resource" techniques.

Devices located in wilderness will be removed when determined to be no longer essential. Permanent equipment caches are prohibited within wilderness. Temporary caches must be evaluated using the minimum requirement concept.

All scientific activities, including the installation, servicing, removal, and monitoring of research devices, will apply minimum requirement concepts and be accomplished in compliance with *Management Policies*, director's orders, and procedures specified in the park's wilderness management plan.
(See Studies and Collections 4.2; Social Science Studies 8.11)

6.3.6.2 – Monitoring Wilderness Resources
In every park containing wilderness, the conditions and long-term trends of wilderness resources will be monitored to identify the need for or effects of management actions. The purpose of this monitoring will be to ensure that management actions and visitor impacts on wilderness resources and character do not exceed standards and conditions established in an approved park plan.

As appropriate, wilderness monitoring programs may assess physical, biological, and cultural resources and social impacts. Monitoring programs may also need to assess potential problems that may originate outside the wilderness to determine the nature, magnitude, and probable source of those impacts.

Appendix D—Yosemite Wilderness Hypothetical Example—Benefits and Impacts Assessment Worksheets

The following benefits and impacts assessment worksheets are an example of a hypothetical proposed scientific study in Yosemite Wilderness. The red boxes on the worksheets show the agency staff evaluations of the benefits and impacts for the hypothetical scientific activity described below. The rationale for the benefits weighting factors and the impact scoring follows each worksheet. Blank worksheets that staff could modify for their own use are provided in Appendix E—details for filling in these benefits and impacts assessment worksheets are given at the beginning of that appendix.

For this hypothetical example, the proposed scientific activity is to install five meteorological sampling stations in Yosemite Wilderness located at different elevations to track climate change effects on temperature, precipitation, and a variety of other weather data. The stations will be used in conjunction with long-term studies on trends in the occurrence of plant and animal species in the area of the weather stations. Each station is relatively conspicuous with a 10-ft high tower and 3- by 3-ft solar panels to power the station and batteries used to store the data for a year. The weather stations will be backpacked in and set up by a team of five people in one day. A research team of five people will camp in the general area of the station for five days to record plant and animal occurrences and conduct maintenance on the weather stations as needed. This team will visit each of the five stations once per year. The intent is to conduct this research every year for 20 years and then leave the meteorological stations in place for the foreseeable future. This research plan will result in a total of 190 person-days of use the first season, and then 175 person-days per season thereafter (including backpacking time into and out from the sites; 5 people x 7 days x 5 sites). (This terse description is insufficient for a real proposal, but is sufficient for the purpose of illustrating how these worksheets are used.)

USDA Forest Service Gen. Tech. Rep. RMRS-GTR-234WWW. 2010

40

Yosemite Wilderness Hypothetical Example — Benefits Assessment Worksheet (CONTINUED)

Date _____ Application # _____ Name _____ Topic _____

Benefit Category	Numerical Score of Benefit (0 = no benefit, 10 = high benefit)						Score	Weighting Factor	Row Total
	0	2	4	6	8	10			
Benefits to Stewardship:									
Would the results address an *urgent* stewardship issue?	Not urgent	Not urgent now but might be in the future	Urgent now but threat or issue appears to be static or decreasing	Urgent now and threat or issue likely to continue at its current state	Urgent now and threat or issue likely to accelerate	Present crisis that may be at the point of irreversibility	8	1.8	14.4
Would the results address an *important* stewardship issue?	Not important	Not important but might be in the future	Important but occurs over a relatively small area or timeframe	Important and occurs over a relatively large area or long timeframe	Important, affecting one or more key biophysical or social aspects over a large area or long timeframe; potential concern for human health/safety	Important, affecting irreversible changes to key biophysical or social aspects over a large area or long timeframe; major concern for human health/safety	6	2.0	12.0
Would the results be applicable *immediately* to stewardship?	Basic research that does not appear to be applicable to a current stewardship issue	Basic research that has slight apparent applicability to a current stewardship issue	Basic research that has moderate apparent applicability to a current stewardship issue	Applied research that has slight to moderate apparent applicability to a current stewardship issue	Applied research that has moderate to high apparent applicability to a current stewardship issue	Research is specifically designed to answer a current stewardship issue	0	0.8	0
Would the results likely be applicable to *future* stewardship issues?	Basic research that is highly unlikely to be applicable in the future	Basic research that is unlikely to be applicable in the future	Research that is unlikely to be applicable in the future except as a baseline to assess future change	Research is moderately likely to be applicable in the future	Research is likely to be applicable in the future	Research is highly likely to be applicable in the future	4	0.6	2.4
Would the results allow *effective action* on a stewardship issue?	Managers would likely not be able to take any actions that affect the issue	Managers could affect the issue only by trying to influence broad societal changes	Managers could take effective action only by changing management priorities	Managers could take effective action only with significant costs to other wilderness values	Managers could take effective action with minimal cost to other wilderness values	Managers could easily and immediately take effective action with no cost to other wilderness values	0	0.3	0
Would the results improve stewardship of this *local wilderness?*	Results are not applicable to the wilderness in which the research is conducted	Results are slightly applicable to the wilderness in which the research is conducted	Results are slightly to moderately applicable to the wilderness in which the research is conducted	Results are moderately applicable to the wilderness in which the research is conducted	Results are highly applicable to the wilderness in which the research is conducted	Results are specifically applicable to the wilderness in which the research is conducted	10	0.7	7.0

Benefit Category	Numerical Score of Benefit (0 = no benefit, 10 = high benefit)						Score	Weighting Factor	Row Total
	0	2	4	6	8	10			
Benefits to Science:									
How broad *geographically* will the results benefit science?	Results benefit science in only a small geographic area or portion of the wilderness	Result benefit science in the whole wilderness	Results benefit science in the whole region	Results benefit science in the whole country	Results benefit science in similar bioregions globally	Results benefit science across the entire planet	4	0.6	2.4
How far over *time* will the results benefit science?	Results provide a short term benefit	Results provide a short to moderate term benefit	Results provide a moderate term benefit	Results provide a moderate to long term benefit	Results provide a long term benefit	Results provide a permanent benefit	8	0.2	1.6
How many different *people* or types of people will benefit from the results?	Results benefit only a few scientists and managers	Results benefit only visitors, scientists, or mangers in the specific wilderness	Results benefit visitors, scientists, and managers in any wilderness	Results benefit local visitors, residents, scientists, and managers	Results benefit regional visitors, residents, scientists, and managers	Results benefit people nationally or globally	8	0.8	6.4
How *important* is the activity to the scientific field of study?	Similar research has been conducted many times before and attempts to answer relatively trivial questions	Similar research has been conducted many times before and attempts to answer relatively minor questions	Research expands slightly on previous work and attempts to answer relatively minor questions	Research expands significantly on previous work and attempts to answer major questions	Research is groundbreaking or precedent setting for the field and attempts to answer major questions	Research is groundbreaking or precedent setting for the field and attempts to answer fundamental questions	6	1.6	9.6
What is the *breadth* of scientific inquiry?	Research is conducted on a single, minor component of the ecosystem or social system with little affect on other components	Research is conducted on a single component of the ecosystem or social system with little affect on other systems	Research is conducted on a single process of the ecosystem or social system that affects a moderate number of other components	Research is conducted on a single process of the ecosystem or social system that affects many components	Research is conducted on many ecosystem or social processes and components	Research is conducted on ecosystem or social processes and components comprehensively	6	0.6	3.6

Total Benefits Assessment Score = 60

Benefits Assessment (Low, Medium, High) = Med

Yosemite Wilderness Hypothetical Example Rationale for Benefits Assessment Worksheet Weighting Factors

The rationale used for the benefits weighting factors is a crucial part of the assessment process. These weights are also important for communicating with others about the professional judgments made in evaluating the benefits of the proposed activities. As an example, the following rationale is provided to explain how the weighting factors in the above Benefits Assessment Worksheet were derived for Yosemite Wilderness—different wilderness staffs would most likely develop different rationales from those given here. Similarly, their resultant scoring would reflect local conditions and attitudes.

Benefits to Stewardship

Would the results address an important stewardship issue? Following Howard Zahniser's wilderness stewardship dictum "managed to be left unmanaged," many people view stewardship primarily as a response to threats to wilderness character. This category is given the highest weight because it directly addresses our obligation under the Wilderness Act to preserve wilderness character.

Would the results address an urgent stewardship issue? The urgency of a threat should obviously affect our response to it, including the benefit of any research that informs our response. Our ability to respond quickly to a threat may affect not only impacts to wilderness character, but the amount of management needed in the future. For example, a quick response to an invasive exotic species can have this double benefit. This double benefit results in a high weight for this factor.

Would the results be applicable immediately to stewardship? This factor assesses a quality of the research results rather than the qualities of the threat. Research that isn't designed to answer specific stewardship questions often produces results that are insufficient to make stewardship decisions. While this is important, it doesn't derive directly from the Act as do the two factors with high weights.

Would the results improve the stewardship of this local wilderness? Again, this assesses the quality of the results more than the nature of the threat. Local applicability is obviously important, but is more of a bonus compared to the overall applicability reflected in the combination of all six "benefits to stewardship" factors. As such, it is given a medium weight.

Would the results likely be applicable to future stewardship issues? While this is obviously not as important as results that would be immediately applicable, it still warrants a medium weight. Basic research may be useful in the future, as scientific knowledge is cumulative.

Would the results allow effective action on a stewardship issue? The relatively low weighting for this factor reflects that there is some benefit from understanding a threat to wilderness character even if the research provides results that do not allow effective management action.

Benefits to Science

How important is the activity to the scientific field of study? This is the only factor that was given a high weight, as it gets to the heart of the purpose of scientific inquiry: the advancement of knowledge.

How many different people or types of people will benefit from the results? As a measure of the breadth of the benefit, this factor merits a medium score because as more types of people are interested in the results, the more potential uses they have. Of the three factors related to the breadth of the results, this one was given slightly greater weight to reflect the direct link to the results being used.

How broad geographically will the results benefit science? As another measure of the breadth of the benefit, this factor also merits a medium weight because research can have greater benefit if it improves our understanding across a larger area.

What is the breadth of scientific inquiry? The last measure of the breadth of the benefit, this factor also merits a medium weight recognizing the importance of synthetic, generalist research that helps us understand whole systems.

How far over time will the results benefit science? This factor was assigned the smallest weight. While it matters that results may be beneficial to science for a long time, the importance and breadth of the results were considered to be far more important than how quickly the information may become obsolete.

USDA Forest Service Gen. Tech. Rep. RMRS-GTR-234WWW. 2010

44

Yosemite Wilderness Hypothetical Example — Impacts Assessment Worksheet

Date _____ Application # _____ Name _____ Topic _____

Impact Category	0	1	2	3	5	10	+	Score
Untrammeled Quality								
Manipulation	None	Slight			Moderate		Large	0
Risk of Unintended Effects	None	Slight			Moderate		Large	1
Disturbance	None		Small		Moderate		Large	0
Natural Quality								
Collection Scarring: Unobtrusive	None	Small amt, short dur	Mod amt, short dur / Sml amt, mod dur	Lrg amt, short dur / Mod amt, mod dur / Sml amt, long dur	Lrg amt, mod dur / Mod amt, long dur	Lrg amt, long duration		0
Collection Scarring: Obtrusive	None			Sml amt, short dur	Mod amt, short dur / Sml amt, mod dur / Sml amt, long dur	Lrg amt, mod dur / Mod amt, long dur	Lrg amt, long duration	0
Collection Scarring: Very Obtrusive	None			Sml amt, short dur	Mod amt, short dur / Sml amt, mod dur	Lrg amt, short dur / Mod amt, mod dur / Sml amt, long dur	Lrg amt, mod duration / Mod or Large amt long dur	0
Collection: Amount and Rarity	None	Any amount, common	Sml amt, uncommon	Mod amt, uncommon	Lrg amt, uncommon / Sml amt, of concern	Mod amt, of concern / Sml amt, rare	Lrg amt, of concern / Med or large amount, rare	0
Undeveloped Quality								
Transport	Human only	1-12 stock days	13-60 stock days	61-90 stock days / 1-10 wheeled days	91-150 stock days / 10-15 wheeled days	151-300 stock days / 16-30 wheeled days / 1 motorized use	+1 each addtl 30 stock days / +1 each addtl 3 wheel days / +10 each addtl motor use	0
Equipment	None	Any amount of unobtrusive use	Any amount of less obtrusive use	1-10 days of ob use	11-30 days ob use / 1 day very ob use	30+ days ob use / 2 days very ob use	+5 each day very ob use	2
Installations: Barely Discernable	None	1-50, short duration	1-40, mod duration / 1-20, long duration	51-150, short dur	151-250, short dur / 61-100, mod dur / 31-50, long dur	251-500, short dur / 101-200, mod dur / 51-100, long dur	+1 each addtl 50 short dur / +1 each addtl 20 mod dur / +1 each addtl 10 long dur	0
Installations: Unobtrusive	None			1-10, short duration	11-50, short dur / 1-10, med dur	51-100, short dur / 11-50, mod dur / 1-10, long dur	+1 each addtl 10 short dur / +1 each addtl 5 mod dur / +1 each addtl long dur	0
Installations: Obtrusive	None			1-3, short duration	4-5, short dur / 1-3, mod dur / 1, long dur	6-10, short dur / 4-5, mod dur / 2-3, long dur	+1 each addtl short dur / +2 each addtl mod dur / +3 each addtl long dur	0
Installations: Very Obtrusive	None					1 short dur	+10 each addtl short dur / +20 each addtl mod dur / +30 each addtl long dur	200
Solitude or Primitive and Unconfined Quality								
Group Size	1-8		8-15	16+ (over limit)				1
Person-Days/Season	1-50		51-150	151+				27
Visitor Surveys	None	Non-Wilderness	Less obtrusive	More obtrusive				0
Surveillance	None	Less obtrusive	Mod obtrusive			Very obtrusive		0

Total Impacts Assessment Score = 231

Impacts Assessment (Low, Medium, High) = High

Yosemite Wilderness Hypothetical Example Rationale for Impact Assessment Worksheet Scores

The rationale used for the numerical scores is a crucial part of communicating with others about the professional judgments made in evaluating proposed activities. As an example, the following rationale is provided for how the numerical scores in the above Impacts Assessment Worksheet were derived for Yosemite Wilderness—different wilderness staffs would most likely develop different rationales from those below. Similarly, their resultant scoring would reflect local conditions and attitudes.

Manipulation—Three broad categories of manipulation are listed. The first category "manipulation" considers manipulation of processes or conditions, with Impact Scores of 2, 5, and +. Area, intensity, and permanence of this manipulation would all be considered. The "slight" impact class might be used to score experimental campsite restoration techniques or trampling studies involving small areas. The "moderate" impact class might be used to score a small experimental prescribed burn. The "high" impact class would be used for studies proposing such actions as the introduction or eradication of species, which may have long-lasting, cascading effects. Scoring for this category is not dependent on whether the proposed manipulation is attempting to increase the health or naturalness of the ecosystem. The high scores associated with impact classes for this category reflect the primacy of untrammeled wilderness in the Wilderness Act.

The second manipulation category is "risk of unintended effects" with Impact Scores of 1, 5, and +. Risk in terms of area, intensity, and permanence of the potential effect would be considered as well as the risk. A proposal may receive a score for this parameter even if no intentional change is planned. One example might be high-risk animal captures of a rare species.

Both of the above categories should also consider the impact to the future scientific value of wilderness. Much of the scientific value of wilderness lies in its untrammeled state and manipulation reduces that value.

The third broad category is "disturbance" with Impact Scores of 2, 5, and +. This usually involves manipulating individual organisms or specific areas rather than processes or conditions and is often more of an impact to the social and symbolic values of wilderness than to ecological or scientific values. This may include such activities as feeding, trapping, sampling, marking, banding, collaring, or instrumenting animals. It may also include disturbance of particularly symbolic entities such as very old or iconic trees, large rare fierce predators, other iconic or historic features, or areas or species sacred or otherwise of cultural importance to local Native Americans.

Two aspects of disturbance would be considered. The first is the magnitude or intensity of insult and attempts to gauge the reduction of wildness to the individual, the reduction of the power of the symbol of wildness, and the sacrilege to sacred places or species that would result from the proposed activity. The second component in this category considers the amount disturbed—this

USDA Forest Service Gen. Tech. Rep. RMRS-GTR-234WWW. 2010

46

would be considered both absolutely and as a percentage of population size. Due to the abstract nature of this category, the condition classes are purposefully left vague. One useful way to consider scoring this category might be to consider the amount of protest that would ensue if the proposal were publicized.

Collection—Impact Scores for this category are 1, 2, 3, 5, 10, and +. Collecting involves removing materials, both living and non-living, from the area for studies or documentation. Three different aspects are considered:

- Scarring—collection sometimes leaves a scar, such as tree notches or bedrock drill holes. Scarring is considered separately from the actual collection and is scored by obtrusiveness, permanence, and amount. Some research may involve scarring that is not incidental to collecting; that is scored here as well.

- Rarity—rarity is a complex topic because a particular resource may be globally, regionally, or locally rare; it may be endemic or non-endemic; it may face various types of threats; and it may be distributed in ways that make it more or less vulnerable. All of these factors should be considered when assigning scores for collecting. Rarity is divided into four broad categories:
  - Common: This would include water, common rocks and soil, and common plants.
  - Uncommon: This would include species at higher trophic levels, including most animals.
  - Of concern: Not rare, but might be at risk or is a member of a declining population, or of particular importance to ecosystem health. This could include species with unknown local population size.
  - Rare: The high scores for the rare category reflect the seriousness of removing rare species or materials from the ecosystem. The rare category includes more than just listed species; a species may be only locally rare, or it may be moderately common locally but threatened or declining at a larger scale—it would still be scored as rare.

- Amount—the impact classes are intentionally left vague as the amount is somewhat dependent on rarity. Amount should be considered both absolutely and as a percentage of population size. An unknown population size (for instance, a research proposal that entails collecting two of every species regardless of rarity, including possible new species) would be scored as "of concern" or "rare." As with the transport and equipment categories below, more than one column may be appropriate, in which case the individual column scores are summed to obtain the total.

Transport—Impact Scores for this category are 0, 1, 2, 3, 5, 10, and + to represent the range of transportation impacts proposed. The impact score considers both the type and amount of transport used. An impact score of 0 is assigned for walking, and higher values represent increasing levels of impact from the use of packstock, wheeled transportation, such as wheelbarrows or game carts used to transport gear, and motorized transportation, such as helicopters, fixed wing aircraft, motor boats, or snowmobiles.

An impact score of 3 is for any wheeled (but non-motorized) transport, a prohibition under Section 4(c) of the Wilderness Act, and would trigger a Minimum Requirements Analysis. The 10+ category is for motorized mechanical transport (helicopters, ATVs, snowmachines, fixed wing aircraft, and skiffs). Local units need to assign how much more than 10 such an impact ranks because local circumstances such as vegetation and topography vary widely and strongly affect how far noise will travel. Other variables to consider include the height above ground level, intended travel (for example, landing or only flying over), evidence of passage (for example, from snowmobile tracks), enabling legislation that allows flights for other purposes, distance of flights, remoteness, and timing.

The amount of use is considered separately. Human or stock transport usually receives a score of 0, or 1 or 2, respectively. There may be circumstances that rate a higher score, however, such as large amounts of stock use in areas that don't normally receive such use or are particularly vulnerable to the impacts of stock, or where stock is otherwise prohibited. The amount of mechanized transport is counted by the total days of use, while the amount of motorized transport is counted by individual uses; for example, if several flights are conducted during a single day, each would be counted. The difference in counting methods helps reflect the much greater impacts of motorized transport. If more than one mode of transportation is used, more than one column would be checked, with the column scores added together to find the total. For example, if a team of researchers propose to hike in to install an instrument tower using 12 stock days (score: 1) to transport their gear and one helicopter flight (score: 10) to transport the tower itself, the total transport score would be 11.

Equipment—Impact Scores are 1, 2, 3, 5, 10, and +. These scores represent a combination of (1) visibility, (2) sound, and (3) technological sophistication and power leverage. This latter aspect attempts to explain the reason why motorized equipment was included as a Section 4(c) prohibition in the Wilderness Act—wilderness is a place where we are "without our mechanisms that make us immediate masters over our environment" (Zahniser 1956). Impact scores and examples are:

- 1 – non-motorized; small; simple; silent (for example, tape measure or binoculars)
- 2 – non-motorized but larger (e.g., mist net); more noise (e.g., star drill); could include small solid-state electronics
- 3 – electric motor; small, not too loud (e.g., cordless electric drill)
- 5 – louder and/or longer-duration motor (e.g., chainsaw)
- 10 or 10+ – multiple uses of motorized equipment

As with transport, if more than one type of equipment use is proposed, more than one column may be checked, with the column scores added together to find the equipment total.

Installations—Impact Scores are 1, 2, 3, 5, 10, and +. Installations are any plot markers, instruments, clusters of instruments, or structures that are left unattended for more than a few days. These are divided into four categories:

- Barely discernable—includes buried rebar, camouflaged tree tags, and other tiny markers or micro-instruments. While these are installations, this scoring system recognizes that a single installation of this type has a negligible impact by itself. Rather, the impact lies in the cumulative effect of many such installations. Thus, it takes many such installations to rise to the level requiring an MRA.

- Unobtrusive—includes larger instruments and plot markers that are easily visible from a short distance but generally not noticeable from greater distances. This category includes things like rebar with large end caps, PVC wells or piezometers that protrude a foot above the ground surface, or brightly-colored plastic flagging or survey tape, which may be quite small but highly visible.

- Obtrusive—includes larger instruments that are visible from a greater distance such as water or air samplers and medium to large boxes sheltering electronics.

- Very obtrusive—includes clusters of instruments, towers, solar panels and antennas, and buildings. Components that move and are, thereby, eye-catching (e.g., anemometer or wind turbine) will often place an installation into this impact category.

Technological sophistication should also be considered when scoring installations. For example, a small rock cairn or small piece of wood would usually be preferable to a metal or plastic pole for use as a plot marker.

Permanence is grouped into three categories. These categories can be modified for each area, but the following is a good starting point: short duration is up to 1 year; moderate duration is 1 to 5 years; long duration is over 5 years. For simplicity only three categories are used, but this also means that interpolation and extrapolation are often necessary and appropriate. For example, five obtrusive installations that will be in place for only two weeks might score a 3 or 4 rather than a 5, while two obtrusive long-term installations are likely to score higher than 10 if they are intended to be permanent.

Group Size—Impact Scores are 1, 2, and 3 and reflect the typical group size for recreational visitors. Use of "legal limit" is done purposefully to strongly denote that this is a red flag, although it is recognized that there may not be a legal limit in some areas. These condition classes should be determined locally. In all cases, group sizes that exceed the legal limit for recreationists should rate a three.

Total Person-Days—Impact Scores are 1, 2, and 3 and reflect the thinking of local staff about how the people added to the area from scientific activities would affect the number of visitors an area already receives. Some wildernesses operate at their maximum total person-days with recreational visitors alone, so any researchers would either effectively "bump" recreational visitors or increase the maximum allowable person-days. This is very place-specific. For example, Yosemite likely would have relatively high numbers of person-days (1 to 50, 50 to 100, greater than 100) while Glacier Bay would likely have lower numbers (1 to 10, 10 to 20, greater than 20). These scores might increase if a substantial number of person-days were spent in a very remote area.

Visitor Surveys—Impact Scores are 1, 2, and 3. The 1 represents an intrusion, albeit a small one. A greater impact on visitors occurs when the survey is conducted farther from the trailhead or in a more remote area. Other elements may affect the score as well, including the number of visitors interviewed, the typical visitor density in the area, or the length of the interview. Interviews at trailheads and wilderness permit stations may still have an impact on visitor experience, particularly if visitors are asked to record encounters or other variables while in the wilderness.

Surveillance—Impact Scores are 1, 2, and 10 and represent local thinking about how surveillance might reduce visitor's sense of wilderness (for example, unencumbered and free from the constraints of society while visiting wilderness) and freedom from being watched. Three elements are integrated into this impact category: (1) whether the tool to collect data on visitor behavior (a person watching, camera, trail counter) is visible to the visitor, (2) whether a visitor could be identified (for example, from a person watching or from a camera) or not, and (3) whether the tool of surveillance is a person or a machine. Local staffs must decide how these three elements vary and interact to assign the impact scores. For example, some local staffs may assign a visible surveillance tool (that nonetheless cannot discern the identity of individuals) as having less impact than a well-hidden camera that records images in which individuals can be recognized.

Appendix E—Worksheets

Sample worksheets are provided on the following pages for each of the filters in this evaluation framework. These worksheets may be an important part of the administrative record for decisions about proposals for scientific activities inside wilderness. These worksheets should be modified to fit local circumstances and judgments, but should not be modified for individual proposals.

Instructions for Using the Worksheets

Cover Sheet

The intent of the cover sheet is to record basic administrative information about the proposed activity. The "topic(s)" entry is for agency use to summarize the broad types of proposals received, such as "geology," "visitor experiences," "invasive species," or any other category of interest or use to the administering office, to aid in organization.

Initial Review Filter

Questions included in the worksheet likely apply in most wildernesses, but local staffs should review these and delete any that aren't applicable and add any that are. After reviewing the proposal, agency staff would check the appropriate "yes" or "no" box for each question. Any "yes" answers indicate that the proposed scientific activity may raise significant problems and may need to be returned to the scientist with an explanation of the problem, or the proposal would likely require significantly more time to evaluate.

Quality of Proposal Filter

The questions included in the worksheet likely apply in most wildernesses, but local staffs should review these and modify them as appropriate. After reviewing the proposal, agency staff would check the appropriate "yes" or "no" box for each question. Any "no" answers indicate that the proposal is insufficient and may need to be immediately returned to the scientist with an explanation of the problem.

Legal and Policy Filter

The steps included in the worksheet should apply in all wildernesses, but local staff members should still review these steps to make sure they are applicable, and add any steps as appropriate for compliance purposes and for the administrative record. Several of the steps require subjective evaluation, and, in such cases, the rationale needs to be carefully documented, especially for proposals that might be controversial.

Impacts and Benefits Filter

There are two worksheets, one for the benefits assessment and one for the impacts assessment. Once the worksheets are completed, the benefits and impacts decision table is used to determine a provisional decision. Based on the outcome of this decision, the proposal is either returned for revision or is evaluated for its contribution to cumulative impacts. After this cumulative impacts assessment, a final recommendation about the proposal is given to the decision maker.

The benefits and impacts assessment worksheets require substantive staff review and should be revised to be made relevant to the local wilderness. To use these worksheets, local staff would:

1. Prepare the worksheets.
   a. Review the category descriptions (bold text at the left of each row on both worksheets) and modify them as appropriate for their local setting; but, in most cases, the ones offered here should fit.
   b. Review the text descriptions for each level of impact or benefit that are under the numerical scores and modify them to fit local needs. For the benefits assessment worksheet, the text descriptions are written generally and would likely be applicable in most wildernesses. For the impacts assessment worksheet, the text descriptions strongly reflect conditions within the Yosemite Wilderness and *must* be modified to fit the context of the individual wilderness.
   c. For the benefits assessment worksheet only, develop weighting factors that reflect local perceptions about the relative importance for each category (rows in the worksheet). The sum of all 11 weighting factors should equal 10 so that when the scores are multiplied by the weighting factors and summed, the maximum total assessment score cannot be greater than 100. These weights should be developed once to fit local needs and not modified for individual proposals.
   d. Develop the cutoffs for low, medium, and high total benefits and impacts assessment scores. These cutoffs will be used to broadly categorize the benefits and impacts; they should be developed once and not modified for individual proposals.

2. Conduct the assessments.
   a. Reading across each row, circle the appropriate statement for the level of benefit or impact.
   b. From the circled statement, read up the column to derive the numerical score.
   c. Record this number for the row under the column titled "Score."
   d. For the benefits assessment, multiply this score with the weighting factor to derive the row total.
   e. Add all the individual row totals to derive the total assessments score.
   f. Based on the cutoffs identified earlier, assign the overall assessment of low, medium, or high.

The benefits and impacts decision table is used to weigh the expected benefits against the impacts of the scientific activity. Before it can be used, local staff members *must* prepare the table by assigning "Provisional Approval," "Provisional Denial," and "Uncertain" to each of the cells. These assignments are fundamentally subjective, reflecting discussion and consensus among local staff. These assignments should be developed once and not modified for individual proposals.

Last, staff members need to identify the types of cumulative impacts that are relevant to the wilderness and determine how the proposed scientific activity would be evaluated for its potential contribution to these impacts.

USDA Forest Service Gen. Tech. Rep. RMRS-GTR-234WWW. 2010

53

COVER SHEET – PROPOSAL FOR SCIENTIFIC ACTIVITY

Date proposal received:

Wilderness:

Name of agency staff evaluating this proposal:

Application #:

Title of proposal:

Name of person submitting this proposal:

Contact information for this person

      Affiliation:

      Address:

      Phone number:

      Email:

Topic(s):

Final recommendation:

Date of final recommendation:

Record of communication between manager and scientist:

INITIAL REVIEW FILTER – QUESTIONS WORKSHEET

Date_____ Application # _____ Short Title _____

Initial Review Question	Yes or No	
Does the proposal include any activities requiring a use that is legally prohibited by Section 4(c) of the Wilderness Act?	☐	☐
Would the proposed activity degrade wilderness character even if it is legally permitted?	☐	☐
Would the proposed activity likely be controversial with any publics?	☐	☐
Would the proposed activity pose other legal or policy problems?	☐	☐
Would the proposed activity interfere with management operations?	☐	☐
Would the proposed activity pose consultation issues over listed species or cultural and heritage resources?	☐	☐
Would the proposed activity require collecting plants or other natural resources, or the handling or removing of animals, or the introduction of plants or animals into the wilderness?	☐	☐
Would the proposed activity pose timing or location problems, such as occurring in a sensitive area or time for particular species?	☐	☐
Would the proposed activity pose additional impact in an area that already has an unacceptable level of cumulative impacts or is close to an unacceptable level of cumulative impacts?	☐	☐
If the submitter has conducted work in the area before, were there any problems with completing administrative requirements (such as submitting reports, removing installations and other debris from the activity, completing curatorial and specimen documentation requirements) in a timely and professional manner?	☐	☐
OTHER QUESTIONS		

Comments or Notes:

QUALITY OF PROPOSAL FILTER – QUESTIONS WORKSHEET

Date_____   Application # _____   Short Title _____

Quality of Proposal Questions	Yes or No	
Is the proposed scientific activity sufficiently well designed to accomplish its stated purpose, thereby providing the intended benefits to management or science?	☐	☐
Does the proposal describe the potential benefits of the proposed activity in terms of the Benefits Assessment described in the Impacts and Benefits Filter?	☐	☐
Does the proposal describe the potential impacts of the proposed activity in terms of the Impacts Assessment described in the Impacts and Benefits Filter, and show how these will be minimized or mitigated?	☐	☐
Does the proposal describe how the results and any reports will be communicated to local management staff?	☐	☐
OTHER QUESTIONS		

If necessary, describe action taken to ensure independent review of the proposal:

Comments or Notes:

LEGAL AND POLICY FILTER – FLOWCHART WORKSHEET

Date_____ Application # _____ Short Title _____

Step 1: Does the proposed activity include any actions or uses that are prohibited by Section 4(c) of the Wilderness Act?

> If no, skip Steps 2 – 4 and go to Step 5.
> If yes, go to Step 2 and describe the actions or uses:

Step 2: Are the prohibited actions or uses necessary? To answer this question, answer the following the questions:

A. Does the proposed work address an urgent or important health and safety concern?
> If yes, go to Step 5. If no, go to Step 2.B.
> Explanation if there is a health and safety concern:

B. Can the prohibited actions or uses only be conducted inside the wilderness?
> If yes, go to Step 2.D. If no, go to Step 2.C.
> Explanation:

C. If the prohibited actions or uses can be conducted outside the wilderness, will the benefits to wilderness stewardship (i.e., preserving wilderness character) or to science be reduced?
> If yes, go to Step 2.D. If no, deny the proposed work.
> Explanation:

D. Are there any legislated exceptions that allow the actions or uses that would normally be prohibited?
> If yes, go to Step 2.E. If no, still go to Step 2.E.
> Explanation if there is a legislated exception:

E. Will the proposed actions or uses help preserve wilderness character?
> If yes, go to Step 4. If no, go to Step 3.
> Explanation:

Step 3: Return the proposal for revision with an explanation of why it is being returned. The revised proposal should include an explanation of changes. Go back to Step 1 with the revised proposal.

Step 4: Go to the Impacts and Benefits Filter.

Step 5: Is there a restriction in law, policy, or management plan that would prevent the actions or uses, or limit where or when they could be used?

> If yes, go to Step 3. If no, go to Step 4.
> Explanation:

Date _____ Application # _____ Short Title _____

Benefit Category	Numerical Score of Benefit (0 = no benefit, 10 = high benefit)						Score	Weighting Factor	Row Total
	0	2	4	6	8	10			
Benefits to Stewardship:									
Would the results address an *urgent* stewardship issue?	Not urgent	Not urgent now but might be in the future	Urgent now but threat or issue appears to be static or decreasing	Urgent now and threat or issue likely to continue at its current state	Urgent now and threat or issue likely to accelerate	Present crisis that may be at the point of irreversibility			
Would the results address an *important* stewardship issue?	Not important	Not important but might be in the future	Important but occurs over a relatively small area or timeframe	Important and occurs over a relatively large area or long timeframe	Important, affecting one or more key biophysical or social aspects over a large area or long timeframe; potential concern for human health/safety	Important, affecting irreversible changes to key biophysical or social aspects over a large area or long timeframe; major concern for human health/safety			
Would the results be applicable *immediately* to stewardship?	Basic research that does not appear to be applicable to a current stewardship issue	Basic research that has slight apparent applicability to a current stewardship issue	Basic research that has moderate apparent applicability to a current stewardship issue	Applied research that has slight to moderate apparent applicability to a current stewardship issue	Applied research that has moderate to high apparent applicability to a current stewardship issue	Research is specifically designed to answer a current stewardship issue			
Would the results likely be applicable to *future* stewardship issues?	Basic research that is highly unlikely to be applicable in the future	Basic research that is unlikely to be applicable in the future	Research that is unlikely to be applicable in the future except as a baseline to assess future change	Research is moderately likely to be applicable in the future	Research is likely to be applicable in the future	Research is highly likely to be applicable in the future			
Would the results allow *effective action* on a stewardship issue?	Managers would likely not be able to take any actions that affect the issue	Managers could affect the issue only by trying to influence broad societal changes	Managers could take effective action only by changing management priorities	Managers could take effective action only with significant costs to other wilderness values	Managers could take effective action with minimal cost to other wilderness values	Managers could easily and immediately take effective action with no cost to other wilderness values			
Would the results improve stewardship of this *local wilderness?*	Results are not applicable to the wilderness in which the research is conducted	Results are slightly applicable to the wilderness in which the research is conducted	Results are slightly to moderately applicable to the wilderness in which the research is conducted	Results are moderately applicable to the wilderness in which the research is conducted	Results are highly applicable to the wilderness in which the research is conducted	Results are specifically applicable to the wilderness in which the research is conducted			

Benefits to Science:

Benefit Category	Numerical Score of Benefit (0 = no benefit, 10 = high benefit)						Score	Weighting Factor	Row Total
	0	2	4	6	8	10			
How broad *geographically* will the results benefit science?	Results benefit science in only a small geographic area or portion of the wilderness	Result benefit science in the whole wilderness	Results benefit science in the whole region	Results benefit science in the whole country	Results benefit science in similar bioregions globally	Results benefit science across the entire planet			
How far over *time* will the results benefit science?	Results provide a short term benefit	Results provide a short to moderate term benefit	Results provide a moderate term benefit	Results provide a moderate to long term benefit	Results provide a long term benefit	Results provide a permanent benefit			
How many different *people* or types of people will benefit from the results?	Results benefit only a few scientists and managers	Results benefit only visitors, scientists, or mangers in the specific wilderness	Results benefit visitors, scientists, and managers in any wilderness	Results benefit local visitors, residents, scientists, and managers	Results benefit regional visitors, residents, scientists, and managers	Results benefit people nationally or globally			
How *important* is the activity to the scientific field of study?	Similar research has been conducted many times before and attempts to answer relatively trivial questions	Similar research has been conducted many times before and attempts to answer relatively minor questions	Research expands slightly on previous work and attempts to answer minor questions	Research expands significantly on previous work and attempts to answer major questions	Research is groundbreaking or precedent setting for the field and attempts to answer major questions	Research is groundbreaking or precedent setting for the field and attempts to answer fundamental questions			
What is the *breadth* of scientific inquiry?	Research is conducted on a single, minor component of the ecosystem or social system with little affect on other components	Research is conducted on a single component of the ecosystem or social system that little affect on other systems	Research is conducted on a single process of the ecosystem or social system that affects a moderate number of other components	Research is conducted on a single process of the ecosystem or social system that affects many components	Research is conducted on many ecosystem or social processes and components	Research is conducted on ecosystem or social processes and components comprehensively			

Total Benefits Assessment Score = ☐

Benefits Assessment (Low, Medium, High) = ☐

Impacts and Benefits Filter — Impacts Assessment Worksheet

Date _____ Application # _____ Short Title _____

Impact Category	\<br\>0	Numerical Score of Impact (0 = negligible Impact, 10 = high Impact)\<br\>1	2	3	5	10	+	Score
Untrammeled Quality								
Manipulation	None		Slight		Moderate		Large	
Risk of Unintended Effects	None	Slight			Moderate		Large	
Disturbance	None		Small		Moderate		Large	
Natural Quality								
Collection Scarring: Unobtrusive	None	Small amt, short dur	Mod amt, short dur / Sml amt, mod dur	Lrg amt, short dur / Mod amt, mod dur / Sml amt, long dur	Lrg amt, mod dur / Mod amt, long dur	Lrg amt, long duration		
Collection Scarring: Obtrusive	None		Sml amt, short dur	Mod amt, short dur / Sml amt, mod dur	Lrg amt, short dur / Mod amt, mod dur / Sml amt, long dur	Lrg amt, mod dur / Mod amt, long dur	Lrg amt, long duration	
Collection Scarring: Very Obtrusive	None			Sml amt, short dur	Mod amt, short dur / Sml amt, mod dur	Lrg amt, short dur / Mod amt, mod dur / Sml amt, long dur	Lrg amt, mod duration / Mod or Large amt, long dur	
Collection: Amount and Rarity	None	Any amount, common	Sml amt, uncommon	Mod amt, uncommon	Lrg amt, uncommon / Sml amt, of concern	Mod amt, of concern / Sml amt, rare	Lrg amt, of concern / Med or large amount, rare	
Undeveloped Quality								
Transport	Human only	1-12 stock days	13-60 stock days	61-90 stock days / 1-10 wheeled days	91-150 stock days / 10-15 wheeled days	151-300 stock days / 16-30 wheeled days / 1 motorized use	+1 each addtl 30 stock days / +1 each addtl 3 wheel days / +10 each addtl motor use	
Equipment	None	Any amount of unobtrusive use	Any amount of less obtrusive use	1-10 days of ob use	11-30 days ob use / 1 day very ob use	30+ days ob use / 2 days very ob use	+5 each day very ob use	
Installations: Barely Discernable	None	1-50, short duration	1-40, mod duration / 1-20, long duration	51-150, short dur / 41-60, mod dur / 21-30, long dur	151-250, short dur / 61-100, mod dur / 31-50, long dur	251-500, short dur / 101-200, mod dur / 51-100, long dur	+1 each addtl 50 short dur / +1 each addtl 20 mod dur / +1 each addtl 10 long dur	
Installations: Unobtrusive	None			1-10, short duration	11-50, short dur / 1-10, mod dur	51-100, short dur / 11-50, mod dur / 1-10, long dur	+1 each addtl 10 short dur / +1 each addtl 5 mod dur / +1 each addtl long dur	
Installations: Obtrusive	None			1-3, short duration	4-5, short dur / 1-3, mod dur / 1, long dur	6-10, short dur / 4-5, mod dur / 2-3, long dur	+1 each addtl short dur / +2 each addtl mod dur / +3 each addtl long dur	
Installations: Very Obtrusive	None					1 short dur	+10 each addtl short dur / +20 each addtl mod dur / +30 each addtl long dur	
Solitude or Primitive and Unconfined Quality								
Group Size		1-8	8-15	16+ (over limit)				
Person-Days/ Season		1-50	51-150	151+				
Visitor Surveys	None	Non-Wildemess	Less obtrusive	More obtrusive				
Surveillance	None	Less obtrusive	Mod obtrusive			Very obtrusive		

Total Impacts Assessment Score = ☐

Impacts Assessment (Low, Medium, High) = ☐

IMPACTS AND BENEFITS FILTER — EXPLANATION OF ASSESSMENT SCORES WORKSHEET

Explanation of Benefits Assessment Scores

Benefits to Stewardship:

Benefits to Science:

Explanation of Impacts Assessment Scores

Impacts to the Untrammeled Quality:

Impacts to the Natural Quality:

Impacts to the Undeveloped Quality:

Impacts to the Solitude or Primitive and Unconfined Quality:

USDA Forest Service Gen. Tech. Rep. RMRS-GTR-234WWW. 2010

61

IMPACTS AND BENEFITS FILTER — BENEFITS AND IMPACTS DECISION TABLE WORKSHEET

Date_____   Application # _____   Short Title _____

		BENEFITS		
		Low	Medium	High
IMPACTS	Low			
	Medium			
	High			

In the prepared Benefits and Impacts Decision Table (see instructions), circle the intersection between the assigned benefits and impacts assessments.

If "Provisional Denial," return the proposal for revision with an explanation of why it is being returned.
Explanation:

If "Provisional Approval," go to the Cumulative Impacts Assessment.

If "Uncertain," discuss concerns with other management staff (as needed) and the scientist to determine if the benefits and impacts were properly assessed, re-assess the proposal if needed, then go to the Cumulative Impacts Assessment.
Explanation:

IMPACTS AND BENEFITS FILTER — CUMULATIVE IMPACTS ASSESSMENT WORKSHEET

Step 1: Are the additional impacts of the proposed scientific activity acceptable when viewed in the context of all the other impacts in the wilderness?
If yes, the proposed activity is recommended for approval. If no, go to Step 2.
Explanation:

Step 2: Return the proposal for revision with an explanation of why it is being returned.
Explanation:

www.ingramcontent.com/pod-product-compliance
Lightning Source LLC
Chambersburg PA
CBHW081240280526
45787CB00006B/2743